From Your Friends At **The MAILBOX® Magazine**

DECEMBER

A MONTH OF IDEAS AT YOUR FINGERTIPS!

GRADES 4–6

WRITTEN BY
Becky Andrews, Casimir Badynee, Tammie Boone, Chris Christensen, Irving P. Crump, Ann Fisher, Beth Gress, Peggy W. Hambright, Paula Holdren, Simone Lepine, Elizabeth Lindsay, Thad H. McLaurin, Mary Lou Schlosser, Christine A. Thuman

EDITED BY
Becky Andrews, Lynn Bemer Coble, Carol Rawleigh, Jennifer Rudisill, Gina Sutphin

ILLUSTRATED BY
Jennifer T. Bennett, Cathy Spangler Bruce, Teresa Davidson, Clevell Harris, Rebecca Saunders, Barry Slate, Donna K. Teal

COVER ART BY
Jennifer T. Bennett

©1996 by THE EDUCATION CENTER, INC.
All rights reserved except as here noted.

Except as provided for herein, no part of this publication may be reproduced or transmitted in any form or by any means, electronic or mechanical, including photocopying, recording, or storing in any information storage and retrieval system or electronic on-line bulletin board, without prior written permission from The Education Center, Inc. Permission is given to the original purchaser to reproduce patterns and reproducibles for individual classroom use only and not for resale or distribution. Reproduction for an entire school or school system is prohibited. Please direct written inquiries to The Education Center, Inc., 1607 Battleground Avenue, Greensboro, NC 27408-8005. The Education Center®, *The Mailbox*®, and the mailbox/post/grass logo are trademarks of The Education Center, Inc., and may be the subject of one or more federal trademark registrations. All other brand or product names are trademarks or registered trademarks of their respective companies. Printed in the United States of America.

TABLE OF CONTENTS

December Calendar 3
Highlight special December days with sensational activities.

December Planner Pages 5
Be prepared for a great month with these handy reproducibles.
Includes:
- A teacher's resource list of December's special days
- December clip art
- An open December newsletter to keep parents informed
- A reproducible calendar of free-time activities for students
- A reproducible award and a student desktag

The Most Wonderful Time! 10
Celebrate the holiday season with a festive collection of activities that spread Christmas cheer across the curriculum!

Folklore Across America 28
Introduce students to the legendary likes of Paul Bunyan, John Henry, Jack, and other American folktale characters with fun thematic activities.

Eight Nights, Eight Lights 40
Shed light on the wonderful traditions of Hanukkah with a collection of fun-to-do activities.

Let Freedom Ring! 46
Examine the events and issues that characterize the Bill of Rights with a cross-curricular unit on freedom.

A Winter Wonderland 60
Welcome the winter season with learning activities that warm up even the frostiest school day.

Gumption, Grit, And A Goal 70
Tickle imaginative minds with a creative collection of activities on inventors and inventing.

Kwanzaa Time! 84
Examine a traditional African-American celebration with teaching ideas that focus on the inspiring holiday of Kwanzaa.

Answer Keys 95

December Calendar

Safe Toys And Gifts Month

Every December, Prevent Blindness America puts out a list of the top ten toys that are hazardous to children's eyesight. Have students create their own top ten lists of toys dangerous to children's eyesight. Discuss their lists; then ask what precautions can be taken by parents and children to prevent injuries from occurring.

Bingo's Birthday Month

In 1929 Edwin S. Lowe manufactured the first bingo game. Today bingo helps numerous charities raise over five billion dollars yearly at fund-raisers. Celebrate bingo's birthday by playing bingo with your students. After playing the original game, play variations—such as Multiplication or Division Bingo—by calling out the facts and having students cover the answers on their boards. Have students create their own versions for other content areas; then let them present and explain their games to the class.

5—International Volunteer Day

International Volunteer Day For Economic And Social Development (sponsored by the United Nations) urges governments to take measures to heighten awareness of the important contribution of volunteer service. Have students discuss the importance of volunteers in the community and how people benefit from their work. Brainstorm ways people can volunteer in their community; then list ways that the students can volunteer for their school (recycling, picking up litter, reading to the younger students). Finally have students decide which item on the list they want to do as a class for your school.

10—Human Rights Day

On this day in 1948, the United Nations developed the Universal Declaration Of Human Rights—an international definition of rights for humankind. Ever since, this day has been known as Human Rights Day. Have students list rights they think every human should have. Ask the students if they have read about any countries in the news where human rights are not guaranteed. Have each student write a short paragraph explaining whether or not the United States should help people of other countries whose human rights are not protected.

14—Birthday Of Nostradamus

Nostradamus was a French doctor born in 1503. He is famous for his astrological predictions. Some people believe his predictions foretold the future. In preparation for the approaching New Year's Day, have your students write on index cards predictions about what will happen around the world by the end of the school year. Collect the cards and put them away until June; then reread them to see which predictions came true.

(Turn the page for more…)

16 — Boston Tea Party Anniversary

On this day in 1773, American patriots dressed as Indians boarded British ships docked in Boston Harbor and dumped 340 crates of tea into the water. This was in protest of a tea tax. Have students brainstorm a list of ways people can protest something they feel is unjust (boycott, petition, march with signs, etc.). Divide the students into groups of two or three. Have each group pick something it would like to protest. Instruct the groups to create posters stating what they are protesting, why they are protesting, and how they are going to peacefully protest.

18 — 13th Amendment Anniversary

The 13th Amendment to the Constitution was ratified on this day in 1865, abolishing slavery in the nation. There were many famous *abolitionists* (people opposed to slavery) whose efforts helped pass the 13th Amendment, such as William Lloyd Garrison, Lucretia Mott, Frederick Douglass, and Sojourner Truth. Have the students work in pairs to select and research one abolitionist. Let each pair share the major accomplishments of its abolitionist and the risks he or she took.

Underdog Day

This holiday (celebrated annually on the third Friday in December) honors all the unsung heroes and Number Two people who contribute so much to the Number One people we read about. Have the students brainstorm a list of people who have contributed to their success at school, home, sports, etc. Then have each student pick one person off the list to honor. Have the student create an Unsung Hero Award stating the person's name and his or her accomplishment. Display the awards on a bulletin board.

27 — Birthday Of Louis Pasteur

Louis Pasteur—born on this day in 1822—pioneered the discovery and control of bacteria, and helped develop immunizations, pasteurization, and a cure for rabies. Have students save their milk cartons from lunch. Write the word *pasteurization* on the board. Have students guess what the word means; then have them look for it on their milk cartons. Tell students that pasteurization is the process of using heat to kill harmful germs. Have students discuss why milk would need to be pasteurized and how bacteria can be helpful to humans (vaccinations, medications, etc.).

30 — Birthday Of Rudyard Kipling

Rudyard Kipling—born on this day in 1865—was a poet, novelist, and Nobel Prize laureate. However, your students will know him better as the author of the *Jungle Books,* "Rikki-Tikki-Tavi," and the *Just-So Stories.* Kipling drew on his childhood in India as the son of a British official for many of his stories. To celebrate his birthday, share some of his works with students or show one of the many movie versions of the *Jungle Books.*

Teacher's December Resource Calendar
A Handy List Of Special Days

December is one of the longest months of the year. It once was one of the shortest with 29 days, until Julius Caesar added two more days. Originally, December was the tenth month of the early Roman calendar. *Decem* is Latin for "ten."

1 — On this day in 1955, Rosa Parks was arrested in Montgomery, Alabama, for refusing to give up her seat and move to the back of a bus.

2 — At age 61, Barney C. Clark became the first person to receive an artificial heart on this day in 1982. He died on March 23, 1983, almost 112 days after receiving the heart.

3 — The United Nations has proclaimed this day International Day Of Disabled Persons.

5 — The pioneer animator and creator of Mickey Mouse—Walt Disney—was born on this day in 1901.

7 — Pearl Harbor Day commemorates the nearly 3,000 people killed during the Japanese attack on Pearl Harbor, Hawaii, in 1941.

12 — On this day in 1901, the first radio signal was sent across the Atlantic Ocean from Cornwall, England, to Newfoundland, Canada, by Guglielmo Marconi.

13 — On this day in 1577, Sir Francis Drake began his three-year voyage around the world.

14 — Roald Amundsen was the first person to reach the South Pole on this day in 1919.

15 — Alexandre Gustave Eiffel—engineer and designer of the Eiffel Tower in Paris, France—was born on this day in 1832.

16 — Composer Ludwig van Beethoven was born in Germany on this day in 1770.

17 — Wright Brothers Day is celebrated on this day. In 1903 Orville and Wilbur Wright successfully flew the first powered airplane near Kitty Hawk, North Carolina.

21 — The first day of winter begins on this day.

23 — Dick Rutan and Jeana Yeager completed the first nonstop flight around the world without refueling on this day in 1987.

30 — The iron ship USS *Monitor*—famous for its Civil War battle with the *Merrimac*—sank off the coast of North Carolina on this day in 1862.

©1996 The Education Center, Inc. • *DECEMBER* • TEC201

December Clip Art
Use on the following items:

- letters to parents
- games
- nametags
- notes to students
- homework assignments
- newsletters
- awards
- learning centers
- bulletin boards

CLASSROOM TIMES

Teacher: _____ Date: _____

DECEMBER

Highlights

Don't Forget!

Hats Off To...

Special Events

Help Wanted

FREE-TIME FUN for December!

Tackle these 20 terrific tasks when you finish your work.

Monday	Tuesday	Wednesday	Thursday	Friday
December 1–7 is Deaf Heritage Week. Learn how to spell your name in sign language.	December 2 is National Roof-Over-Your-Head Day. List five ways you can help the homeless in your community.	Where do all the missing pencils go? Are they stolen or do they sprout legs and run away? Write a story to explain.	Tell Someone They're Doing A Good Job Week is in December. Write a note of praise to a hard worker in the class. *Great job, Carlos!*	Get ready early and make a New Year's resolution. Write down something you want to change or improve about yourself.
Some countries use only coins for money. List some advantages to having only coin money?	List the letters in *December* in a column. Write a word that describes December for each letter. *D*elicious *E*lves *C*old	Most think of turkey or ham when planning a holiday meal. Create a unique and unusual main dish for your holiday meal.	December is full of wonderful foods. Make a menu of your favorite holiday meal.	How are a hammer and a computer alike?
Palindromes are words that are the same forward and backward. How many palindromes can you think of? DAD RADAR EVE	List as many holidays as you can that take place in December. 1. Christmas 2. Hanukkah	December usually brings the first snow storms. Describe the last snow storm you remember.	It is better to give than to receive. Describe a time when you gave and felt really good about it.	There are a lot of holiday symbols. Create a new holiday symbol that represents peace, love, and harmony.
Look at a one-dollar bill closely. Do you see the spiderweb spun all over the front? Can you find the spider that spun the web?	Describe the most unusual thing you've eaten for breakfast.	Humbug Day is December 21. This is a day to vent all your holiday frustrations. Make a list of your frustrations and share it with your neighbor. *Bah, Humbug!*	Many families have holiday traditions. Write about one of your family traditions that is special to you.	December 31 is You're All Done Day. Make a list of all your accomplishments for the past year. 1.___ 2.___ 3.___

©1996 The Education Center, Inc. • *DECEMBER* • TEC201

Note To The Teacher: Have each student staple a copy of this page inside a file folder. Direct students to store their completed work inside their folders.

Patterns

Desktag: Duplicate student copies on construction paper. Have each student personalize and decorate his pattern; then laminate the patterns and use them as desktags during December.

Award: Duplicate multiple copies. Keep them handy at your desk during the month of December. When a student earns an award, write the special activity earned on the appropriate line. Or let the student choose the special activity with your approval.

©1996 The Education Center, Inc.

Two Thumbs Up For Terrific Work!

This entitles you to the following special activity:

To:
From:
Date:

©1996 The Education Center, Inc. • *December* • TEC201

The Most Wonderful Time!

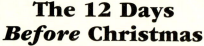

Teaching Ideas For Celebrating The Christmas Season

Like the song says, "It's the most wonderful time of the year!" So celebrate with a host of cross-curricular activities—all designed to keep your excited elves busy and motivated during those long, preholiday school days.

by Chris Christensen

The 12 Days *Before* Christmas

Generate anticipation for the upcoming holiday season with this fun countdown-calendar activity. About 15 school days before the first day of your holiday vacation, make a master copy of the tree pattern on page 20; then copy it on green construction paper for each child. Have each student carefully cut around the dashed line of each ornament on his tree (leaving the solid line at the top intact) and then cut out the tree. Invite students to decorate their trees with glitter, yarn, buttons, or other materials. In addition, provide each student with 12 gummed stars to close the ornament flaps.

Next program your master copy of the pattern with 12 activities for students to complete during the 12 days preceding the holiday. Activities can include writing topics, math problems/puzzles, vocabulary exercises, research questions—anything that will keep students motivated and on-task during these hectic days.

On the 12th day before your holiday vacation begins, have each student align a copy of the programmed tree under his green tree; then have him staple the two together. Direct students to open the flap for ornament 12 and complete its activity. Continue with an ornament per day, counting down to the final school day before the holidays.

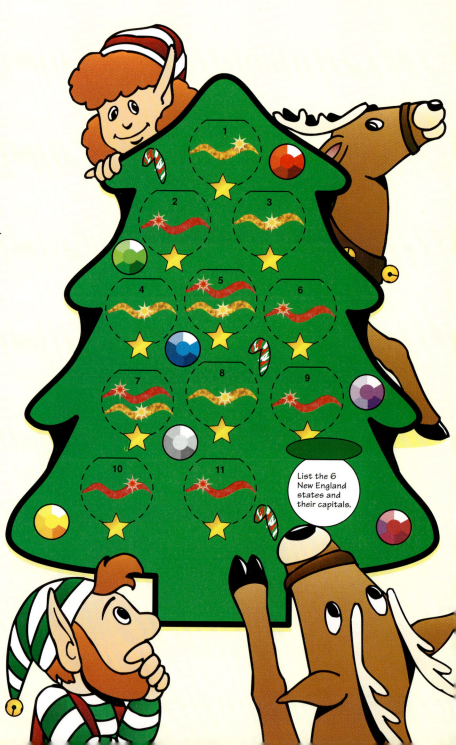

Reindeer Treats

During this time of giving and sharing, have your little dears make these treats for Santa's reindeer—then present the snack to a class of younger children. Divide students into groups of five. Have each group be responsible for obtaining its ingredients and other materials needed.

Reindeer Treats

Ingredients needed (for each group of five):
- 2 cups unflavored oatmeal
- 2 cups bran cereal
- 2 cups shredded coconut
- 2 cups raisins
- 2 cups Grape-Nuts®

Other materials needed:
- large bowl for mixing
- large mixing spoon
- 5 plastic, zippered bags (sandwich size)
- 5 copies of poem on page 21
- 5 lengths of ribbon

Directions:
1. Pour all of the ingredients in a large bowl and mix.
2. Fill each zippered bag with the mixture (about 2 cups).
3. Color and cut out a poem for each bag.
4. Punch a hole in the top middle of each bag and at the dot at the top of the poem.
5. Tie a poem to each bag with ribbon.

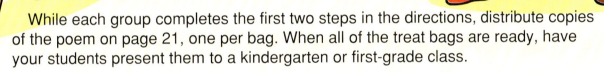

While each group completes the first two steps in the directions, distribute copies of the poem on page 21, one per bag. When all of the treat bags are ready, have your students present them to a kindergarten or first-grade class.

Home For The Holidays

Discuss with students the many sights, sounds, tastes, and smells that they experience during the holiday season. Then have them work independently to make these creative-writing shape booklets. First provide each student with a white, construction-paper copy of the house pattern on page 22. Instruct each student to personalize the house with her family name, then add her favorite decorations: candles in windows, strings of colorful lights, wreaths, etc. Next have each student cut around the bold outline of the house, creating the cover of her "At My Home" holiday booklet.

Every day for several days provide each student with a blank sheet of duplicating paper. First have the student trace her cover on top of the sheet; then have her illustrate a holiday favorite (see the samples) on the top half of the shape. On the bottom half, have the student write a paragraph telling why that particular item is so special. After completing six or seven pages, have each student cut out the house tracings and combine them with her cover to create a take-home booklet of holiday favorites.

O Christmas Tree, O Christmas Tree

One of the season's most common symbols is the Christmas tree. Focus on the popularity of Christmas trees with the following activities.

Christmas: 3001 A.D.

Take your students on a trip into the future! Tell them to pretend that Christmas trees have long been gone due to environmental factors. Divide your class into cooperative groups or pairs and assign each group one of the settings listed below. Direct each group to work together to determine a Christmas tree substitute that takes into consideration its setting's location, climate, available materials, and public interest. Have each group prepare an illustration and oral presentation explaining its choice.

Settings:
- an underwater colony
- a lunar colony
- a desert colony
- a polar colony
- an underground colony
- an orbiting space colony

It's For The Birds

As we decorate our homes and classrooms, we can also look out our windows and see numerous evergreens that have been decorated for the season. This is a perfect springboard for a learning activity that involves nature and a little math fun.

Have your students prepare lots of unsalted popcorn, using either conventional poppers or a microwave oven. Also ask parents for donations of fresh, whole cranberries. Provide each student with a large sewing needle and plenty of thread. Instruct each student to first tie a large knot in one end of his thread. Then have him string the popcorn and cranberries, creating a repeated pattern. When each child has finished his string, ask him to share it with his classmates to see if anyone recognizes the pattern that was created. Next have students tie several strings together and hang the garlands from trees and shrubbery on your campus. And don't forget to make extra popcorn for student munching!

Decorate-The-Tree Game

This simple game is sure to keep the holiday spirit alive in your classroom. Provide each student with a copy of the reproducible game on page 23 and a regular paper clip. Next divide students into groups of two, three, or four to play the game. Each group will need colored pencils, crayons, or colored markers. Direct students to use a paper clip under a pencil tip as a spinner for the game.

Turn this game into a skill game by requiring that a student spell a word, answer a question, or give the answer for a multiplication fact before he spins the spinner. Or use the game as a party-time activity.

Pasta Trees

This pasta tree is an easy-to-make, fun centerpiece to decorate the family dinner table over the holidays. First provide each student with a 9" x 12" sheet of tagboard. Have each student roll his sheet into a cone shape, then staple and tape it so that it retains its shape. Next have each student trim the bottom of the cone so that it will stand level, creating a Christmas-tree shape.

Have each student paint a small section of his tree with glue, then cover it with a variety of pasta shapes. Each section should dry completely before work begins in another area. After the tree shape has been completely covered with pasta and has dried sufficiently, spray-paint it with silver or gold paint. After allowing a day for drying, spray each tree with a clear, polyurethane finish.

Suggest that students display their trees in inexpensive plastic goblets, with bows tied around the bottom as shown.

Get Cracking!

Another holiday season tradition is the presentation of *The Nutcracker,* the world's most popular ballet. Students often hear the wonderful music of Tchaikovsky without realizing that it is from *The Nutcracker* ballet. Why not develop a center based on this holiday story that dates back over a hundred years ago? Below are suggestions for creating a Nutcracker minicenter for your students. To prepare, ask your students and their parents to help you collect the following items for the center:

- an assortment of nutcracker figures, ornaments, and pictures
- a basketful of various kinds of unshelled nuts
- three to five books that tell the story of the Nutcracker (see the suggestions below)
- 2" x 9" white construction-paper strips
- graphing paper
- construction-paper scraps

Next reproduce a supply of activity cards (see the bottom half of page 21). Label the cards with the following activities; then display them on a bulletin board near your center.

Activity Card Tasks:

- Nutcracker figures come in a variety of sizes and can look quite different from one another. Select any two nutcrackers or illustrations of nutcrackers at the center. Compare and contrast them in a Venn diagram.
- Sort the nuts in the basket. Make a graph showing the number of each type.
- Make a pattern using the nuts in the basket. Draw your pattern on a paper strip.
- There are different versions of *The Nutcracker*. Choose one of the books in the center and read it with a partner. Then write a review of the book together.
- The ballet version of *The Nutcracker* was based on a story called *The Nutcracker And The King Of Mice.* Using construction paper, create your own version of the Mouse King and display it at the center.
- Write one more chapter for the book describing what you think happened after Marie woke up.
- Write about and illustrate your favorite part of the story.

Children's Books Based On *The Nutcracker:*
The Nutcracker Ballet by Vladimir Vagin (Scholastic Inc.)
Stories From The Classical Ballet by Belinda Hollyer (Viking)
Of Sugarplums And Satin Slippers by Violet Verdy (Scholastic Inc.)

Special Memories Are Never Forgotten

Of all the holidays of the year, this season maintains the most traditions. Each family seems to do something special that is remembered and possibly repeated year after year. Maybe it's leaving a special treat for the reindeer or perhaps it is a special food that's only prepared during this season.

Share with students some of the classroom traditions that you include during the holiday season year after year. Have students discuss which ones they have enjoyed the most. Next have students share their own personal favorite traditions of the season (other than receiving gifts, of course!). Then prepare students for this assignment, which is actually a family homework task. Explain that each student is to sit down with his family and discuss a special holiday tradition or an occurrence that was enjoyed by the entire family. Provide each student with a copy of the half-page reproducible on the top of page 25 to record the memory. Ask students to return their sheets to class after completing them.

See the following bulletin-board idea for displaying students' special memories.

Special Memories Bulletin Board

Turn the family homework assignment described above into a bulletin board that integrates the Christmas holiday and the diverse backgrounds represented in your classroom. Cover a board with green holiday fabric that has a tiny print. Stretch the cloth to remove any wrinkles before stapling it to the board. Add red lettering and trim. When all of the family homework assignments have been returned and shared, display them on the board along with an enlarged copy of the elephant pattern on the bottom of page 25.

Let's Trim The Tree!

For as long as people have brought evergreen trees into their homes, they have decorated them with candles, cookies, paper, and more. Below and on the next page are four quick tree ornaments that students can make.

Ornament Cubes

Review or introduce the concept of the geometric cube with this fun art project. Duplicate page 24 on white construction paper for each student. Provide glitter, glue, paper clips, assorted markers, and two-inch pieces of pipe cleaners. Then have students follow the steps listed on the page to make their cube ornaments.

To extend this activity, suggest a variety of themes on which students can base their cubes's four illustrations, such as:

- four Christmas carols
- four Christmas symbols
- how four different animals celebrate Christmas
- four different ways to decorate a tree
- four photos (or parts cut from photos)
- illustrations cut from magazine pages
- 3-D decorations (such as sequins, buttons, dry pasta, etc.)

Frame-Ups

This ornament is not only easy to make, but becomes a decorative keepsake to put on the tree each year at Christmastime as well!

Materials:
1 mason jar dome lid (used in canning)
1 red (or green) felt circle the same size as the lid
1 red (or green) felt circle cut to fit the inner circle of the shiny side of the lid
glue
1 five-inch piece of red yarn (or gold thread)
a small facial photo of each child
1 piece of narrow red (or green) ribbon

Directions:
1. Glue each end of the piece of red yarn to the underside of the lid (the side with the rubber seal), creating a loop.
2. Glue the larger red circle to the same side of the lid, securing the yarn and covering the underside of the lid.
3. Glue the smaller circle inside the depression of the shiny side of the lid. This leaves the gold rim showing.
4. Turn the lid so that the piece of yarn extends from the top. Then glue your photo to the felt inside the shiny frame.
5. Glue a small ribbon bow to the top edge.

Decorative Nests For The Tree

Tradition says that a spiderweb or bird's nest in the Christmas tree is a symbol of good luck for the upcoming year. Help your students have a good new year by making these nest ornaments.

Materials:
- a spring-type clothespin, spray-painted red or green
- half of a walnut shell
- a bit of dried moss
- small dried white beans
- glue
- yarn
- red or green construction paper
- rubber cement
- pencil
- two-inch square of white paper
- three-inch square of colored paper
- hole puncher

Directions:
1. Glue some moss inside the walnut shell half to resemble a nest.
2. Glue three or four beans in the nest. Let dry.
3. Glue the walnut shell to the clip end of the clothespin and let it dry.
4. Copy the poem shown on the white-paper square. Add decorations if desired.
5. Rubber-cement the white paper square onto the colored paper square. Punch a hole in the top right corner.
6. Thread the yarn through the wire coil of the clothespin, then through the hole on the card.

*This tiny Christmas nest
Brings more than holiday cheer.
It's sure to bring good luck to you
Throughout the coming year!*

Half-Moon Ornaments

These easy-to-make ornaments will become lasting mementos of your students' school year. Ask each student to bring to school a current school picture or any recent snapshot—as long as the photo is a close-up facial shot. Provide each student with one-half of a Styrofoam® ball (3-inch diameter), glue, and glitter. Instruct each student to glue the photo, trimming it if necessary, to fit in the middle of the flat side of the Styrofoam® hemisphere. Next have each student brush water-thinned glue on the remainder of the flat side and sprinkle on glitter. After this section has dried, instruct each student to add glue and glitter to the rounded side of the ornament. To complete the project, have each student pin a small bow at the top of her photo.

To make a hanger, have each student tie together the ends of a 10-inch length of ribbon, then pin the knotted end to the back of the ornament. It's then ready to take home and display on the tree!

Keeping Track Of Santa's Helpers

The news seems to focus on problems we face each and every day. Use this season of love and giving to identify positive happenings. Create a large poster with the heading "Santa's Helpers Come In All Sizes And Shapes." Display the poster in your classroom. Discuss with students the importance of finding the good in the world around us. Challenge them to watch the news and read newspapers to find acts of kindness that have been featured. Ask students to clip these articles from the newspapers or summarize them in writing. Set aside a time each day for sharing. Then display the articles on the poster. As the poster fills up, you'll surely notice more random acts of kindness occurring in your classroom.

Where'd You Get That Tree?

Send your class on a data-gathering expedition with this simple math activity that reinforces surveying and graphing skills. First have each student fold a sheet of paper into fourths, then unfold it so that it has four sections. Instruct each student to copy the following categories on her paper, one per box:

- bought (or will buy) a cut tree from a lot
- bought (or will buy) a live tree
- used (or will use) an artificial tree
- cut (or will cut) our own live tree

Next have students circulate around the room asking at least 15 classmates to respond to the question, "Where did (or will) your family get your Christmas tree this year?" Instruct each student to use tally marks in each of the boxes to indicate the number of responses. After all surveys have been completed, direct each student to show the information she gathered in either a bar graph or a pictograph.

Need other graphing ideas? Have students survey each other—or other classes—to gather information on the following topics:

- What's your favorite holiday song?
- Do you prefer colored lights or plain white ones?
- What's your favorite Christmas symbol?
- If you could make one Christmas wish for the world, what would it be?
- What's your favorite holiday movie?
- What's your favorite Christmas book or story?
- How many of Santa's reindeer can you name in 20 seconds?

From My House To Yours

Duplicate additional copies of the house pattern on page 22 for a pair of fun student-made projects:

- *For an eye-catching bulletin-board display:* Ask each student to cut a small photo of his family (or one that includes only himself) to fit in the large window (2" x 1 1/2") on the right half of the house. Have each student trim his photo and glue it in the window, then color the rest of the house with colorful lights, candles in windows, wreaths, etc. After students cut out their houses, display the completed projects on a bulletin board titled "From My House To Yours."

- *For a greeting card:* Have each student cut a photo of himself to glue in the window (2" x 1 1/2") on the right side of the house. Next instruct each student to carefully cut out the large picture window on the left side of the house (also 2" x 1 1/2"). Have students use the roof space to add their personal messages. After coloring and cutting out the house, have each student fold the house on its vertical line of symmetry so that the photo is visible through the cut-out window. Instruct each student to decorate the front of the card with a greeting to the person(s) to whom the card will be sent. Instruct each student to mail his card in a business envelope.

Stocking Fillers

Since students love holiday stockings filled with goodies, use this fun activity to review skills that you've already taught. Provide each student with two 9" x 12" sheets of colorful construction paper. Instruct each student to draw a stocking on one sheet so that the top of the stocking is large enough to hold a small index card. After cutting out his stocking, have each student trace it on the second sheet of paper and cut out the copy. Have the student glue the two cutouts together, leaving the top of the stocking open. He can then personalize and decorate the stocking.

Next have each student program 11 small index cards with questions relating to topics you've been studying (math problems, misspelled words, sentences to punctuate, etc.). In addition, have each student label a 12th card with all answer keys.

When everyone has finished creating his card set, have each student exchange cards with a partner (not including the key card). After answering all of the questions on a sheet of paper, each student gives his answers to his partner to be checked. Instruct each student to place all of his partner's cards that have correct answers in the partner's stocking. Have the partners discuss those questions that were answered incorrectly. To play the game again, simply have students pair up with different classmates.

Pattern

Use with "The 12 Days *Before* Christmas" on page 10.

20   ©1996 The Education Center, Inc. • *DECEMBER* • TEC201

Reproducible Poem
Use with "Reindeer Treats" on page 11.

Reindeer Treats

Why is it, oh dear Santa Claus,
It always is just you
Who gets the treats on Christmas Eve,
And never just a few?

Your faithful reindeer guide the way;
They're always filled
With joy!
They also must get hungry
As they visit girls and boys!

So here's a little reindeer treat.
Please feed it to your crew,
And give a kiss to Rudolph,
Dear Santa,
I love you!

©1996 The Education Center, Inc. • *DECEMBER* • TEC201

Reproducible Activity Card
Use with "Get Cracking!" on page 14.

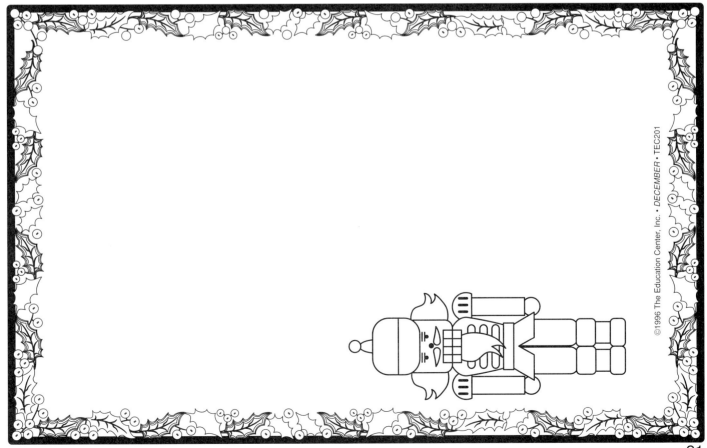

©1996 The Education Center, Inc. • *DECEMBER* • TEC201

Pattern
Use with "Home For The Holidays" on page 11 and "From My House To Yours" on page 19.

Name _____ Gameboard

Decorate-The-Tree Game

How fast can *you* decorate a tree? Play this game with one to three friends. The winner is the first person to completely decorate his tree. When it's your turn, use the spinner to find out what to do.

To use the spinner, place the end of a paper clip at its center. Place your pencil inside the paper clip with its point on the center. Flick the paper clip so that it spins around.

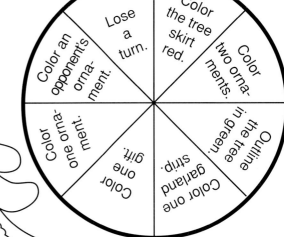

Spinner

©1996 The Education Center, Inc. • *DECEMBER* • TEC201

Note To The Teacher: Use with the idea on page 13.

Name _____

24   Art project

Make A Cube Ornament

Make this three-dimensional ornament to add to your Christmas tree. Just follow the steps below:

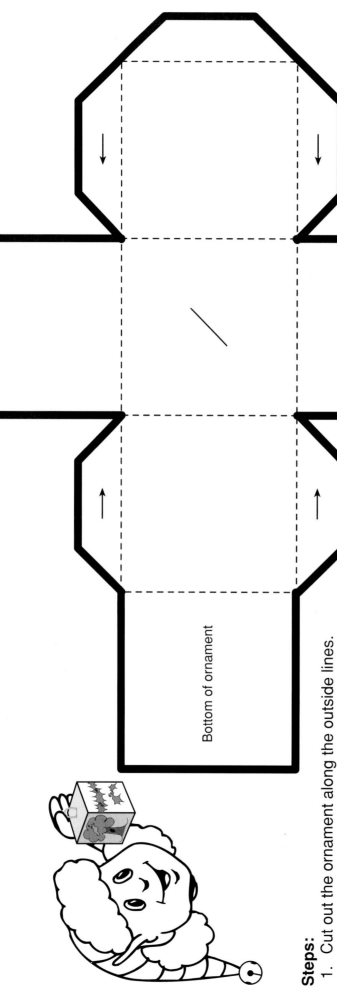

Steps:
1. Cut out the ornament along the outside lines.
2. Make a small slit on the line of the middle square. This square is the top of the cube.
3. Draw a holiday illustration in each of the four other unlabeled squares. Note: the arrows on each square's tabs point toward the top of that square.
4. Fold down at each dashed line. Then fold the tabs inward and glue the cube's sides in place.
5. Tuck the ends of a U-shaped piece of pipe cleaner inside the slit.
6. When the cube is dry, hang it on your Christmas tree!

Note To The Teacher: Use with "Ornament Cubes" on page 16.

©1996 The Education Center, Inc. • *DECEMBER* • TEC201

Pattern
Use with "Special Memories Are Never Forgotten" on page 15.

I Remember When...

A Special Holiday Memory
of the
_____ Family

What?_____
Who?_____
When?_____
Where?_____
This memory is special because _____
_____
_____

_____
_____

©1996 The Education Center, Inc. • DECEMBER • TEC201

Bulletin-Board Pattern
Enlarge this pattern to use with the bulletin board on page 15.

©1996 The Education Center, Inc. • DECEMBER • TEC201

25

Name _____   *Symmetry*

Holiday Symmetry

Oh, no! The Christmas Humbug has stolen half of the illustration below! Only you can get it back! See how well you can re-create the missing half of the picture. Remember to make sure that you match everything, square for square, so that your picture is perfectly symmetrical. Use a pencil to finish the illustration. When you're finished, neatly color it!

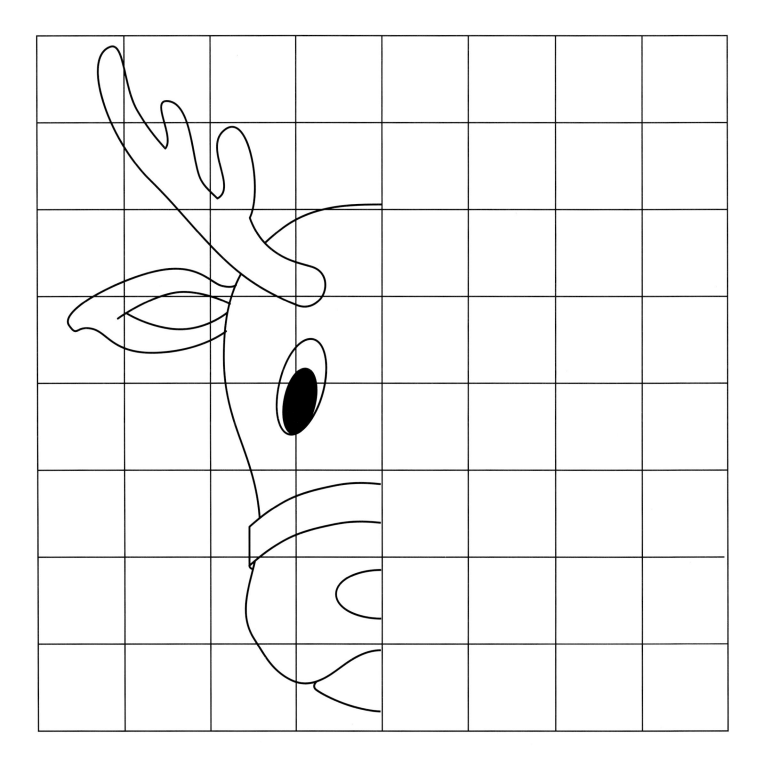

Bonus Box: Use a sheet of graph paper to create your own holiday symmetrical design. Illustrate only half of the design. Then exchange papers with a classmate and complete each other's drawings.

Name _____   Spelling, word play

Christmas Connections

In order for the entire set of lights to come on, each bulb must contain a correct answer! Look at each set of letters below. Each set is really a compound word or pair of words about Christmas. But the two parts of the word pair have been woven together. To solve each one, just separate the two words—without changing the order of any letters. Write each answer in its matching bulb.

Example: 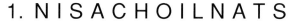 C**MHER**RIST**MRAY**S = Merry Christmas

1. N I S A C H O I L N A T S
2. D R E E I E R N
3. C A C A N N E D Y
4. S C L A N A T U A S
5. W G I R A F P T
6. S L R I E D I G E H
7. F R C U A I K T E
8. B G I R E N G E A R D
9. G E R E V E E R N
10. B E J I L N G L L S E
11. S N I L I E G N H T T
12. M I T S O T L E E
13. C L A I N D G L H E T
14. W H O L R E L A T Y H
15. F A R E M U I N L I Y O N
16. C O C U T O K I T E E R
17. F S L A N O K E W
18. M U C H O S I R I C

Bonus Box: What two-word, old-fashioned Christmas treat can you spell by unscrambling these letters: D I P G U L P M U N D ?

Folklore Across America

For generations American folklore has traveled with its people across the nation. In honor of the December 9 birthday of Joel Chandler Harris—the creator of the Uncle Remus tales—introduce students to the legendary likes of Paul Bunyan and John Henry with rip-roaring activities that match the greatness of these beloved characters.

by Mary Lou Schlosser and Peggy Hambright

Tell Me A Story

Traditionally folktales are passed along by word of mouth. Have students carry on this oral tradition by learning folktales to share with others. Gather picture books from the list provided. Help each student choose one about a favorite character. If two students choose the same tale, it's okay—having at least two versions of the same tale authenticates it as folklore. Simply have one student make his version a variation of the other—another indication of genuine folklore. To help students feel comfortable with their storytelling abilities, give them copies of the guidelines on page 36. Schedule times for your storytellers to tell their tales to audiences of younger students. Be sure to see "Storyteller's Vest" on page 29 for a great prop students can wear while sharing their stories.

American Tall Tales by Mary Pope Osborne (Alfred A. Knopf Books For Young Readers, 1991)

Big Men, Big Country: A Collection Of American Tall Tales by Paul Robert Walker (Harcourt Brace & Company, 1993)

Cut From The Same Cloth: American Women Of Myth, Legend, And Tall Tale by Robert D. San Souci (Putnam Publishing Group, 1993)

John Henry And His Mighty Hammer by Patricia A. Jensen (Troll Associates, 1993)

Johnny Appleseed Goes A' Planting by Patricia A. Jensen (Troll Associates, 1993)

Mike Fink by Steven Kellogg (Morrow Junior Books, 1992)

Paul Bunyan And His Blue Ox by Patricia A. Jensen (Troll Associates, 1993)

Pecos Bill, The Roughest, Toughest Best by Patricia A. Jensen (Troll Associates, 1993)

Sally Ann Thunder Ann Whirlwind Crockett: A Tall Tale by Steven Kellogg (Morrow Junior Books, 1995)

Figures-Of-Speech Scavenger Hunt

American folklore is rich in literary devices—so have students search for them throughout this unit. Divide a bulletin board into six sections: *simile, metaphor, hyperbole, alliteration, onomatopoeia,* and *symbolism*. Let students look in different kinds of dictionaries to find a definition and examples of each figure of speech. Write them under the proper headings. Thumbtack several markers tied to lengths of yarn along the board so students can add new examples—including the references where they were heard or read—as they find them during the unit. With each story students write or tell during the unit, encourage them to use figures of speech too.

Storyteller's Vest

Send your folklore tellers (see "Tell Me A Story" on page 28) off to other classrooms in style with versatile props that can be used later with other types of stories. Just ask students to bring paper grocery bags from home. In the meantime make a pattern for students to trace:

1. Cut along one side of a bag from top to bottom. Cut away the bag's bottom and trim away 1/2-inch of the bag's top edge. Fold the bag in half (printed side in) with its fold to the left (figure 1).
2. On top of the folded paper, draw a pattern similar to figure 2; then cut on the dotted lines where indicated.
3. Open the bag and refold it to make the vest lie as in figure 3. Cut a pocket pattern from any scrap paper.

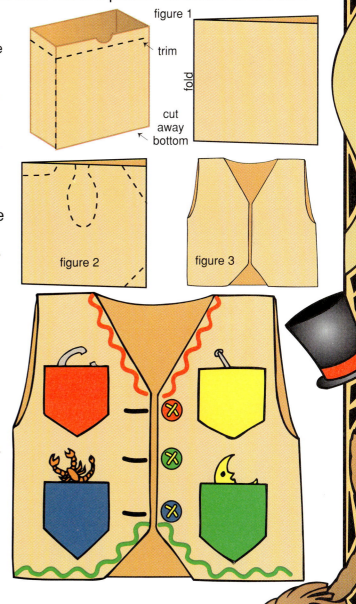

Let students cut and fold their bags like figure 1. Then have them take turns tracing and cutting out their vests using the pattern. Next have them trace and cut out four construction-paper pockets—one each of the following colors: red, green, blue, and yellow. Help students staple the inside shoulder seams and then two pockets on each of the two front sides. Have students use crayons and markers to make decorations that mimic rickrack trim, buttons, etc. Ask each student to fill the pockets with drawings or objects that represent four separate, nonsequential incidents from the story he plans to share. As the storyteller introduces his story to a younger class, he calls on volunteers to choose a pocket by color. He then pulls the object from the pocket and uses it to tell another part of his story. (You may wish to laminate these vests for durability so they can be used throughout the year during other storytelling sessions.)

Tracking American Folklore

Show students the different geographic regions from which American folklore characters originated with an instructional bulletin board. Enlarge a simple outline map of the United States. Have a group of students color its topographical regions. Mount the map on a bulletin board. Duplicate (enlarging if necessary) the tall-tale character symbols on page 39. Select a student to lightly color the symbols and cut them out. Post the symbols on the outline map according to the illustrated board below. Title the board "Folklore Across America." Refer to the board each time a different character is introduced.

Tell Me Why

Some American folktales are myths that attempt to explain why natural events happen. Why does it thunder? Why are there earthquakes? Why are there seasons? Share some stories with students from Gretchen Will Mayo's *Earthmaker's Tales: North American Indian Stories About Earth Happenings* (Walker And Company, 1989). Ask students to brainstorm natural phenomena and then choose one event to explain in a story. Display the completed stories in a class book titled "Just Why Stories."

Clever "Fellers"

Many folktales have animal heroes that act like humans and use their natural traits to deceive or outwit other animals. These stories are collectively called *trickster tales*. Native Americans gave us tales about a raven or a coyote deceiving or being deceived by other animals. African Americans gave us tales about smaller animals outwitting larger and stronger animals. Joel Chandler Harris pitted his Uncle Remus characters—Brer Rabbit, Brer Fox, Brer Bear, and Brer Wolf—against each other in battles of wits.

Share with students Gerald McDermott's *Coyote: A Trickster Tale From The American Southwest* (Harcourt Brace & Company, 1994), several selections from *The Tales Of Uncle Remus: The Adventures Of Brer Rabbit* by Julius Lester (Dial Books For Young Readers, 1987), or stories from Virginia Hamilton's *The People Could Fly: American Black Folktales* (Alfred A. Knopf Books For Young Readers, 1985). Then have students brainstorm a list of animals known by their particular traits—courageous lions, clever foxes, industrious beavers—on which to base their own trickster tales. Have each student research one animal to find out more about its habits. Ask the student to write about the animal's traits and habits in a story in which the animal outwits a person or another animal. Give students lunch-sized bags to decorate and then use for storing their tales. Display the bags on a bulletin board titled "Bags Of Tricksters."

That Boy Named Jack

North Carolina's Appalachian mountain region has given American folklore a universal hero named Jack who uses his common sense to outsmart the meanest of the mean. Share selections from Gail E. Haley's *Mountain Jack Tales* (Dutton Children's Books, 1992) or from Richard Chase's *The Jack Tales* (Houghton Mifflin Company, 1993). As your students become familiar with Jack's goodness and humor, call attention to the mountain dialect characteristic of these tales. Duplicate a short tale from one of the books. Give a copy to each group to read. Have the group highlight examples of dialect; then have them list their ideas as to what the terms mean. Come back together as a class. Discuss the words and how the use of dialect enhances the story and preserve the oral tradition.

Time-Traveling Heroes

What would legendary figures like Stormalong, Mike Fink, or Paul Bunyan do if they were involved in the challenges or hardships of today's world? Ask students to find a news story in which a legendary hero could tackle a current problem with the same courage he did during the time he lived. Have each student glue the news story to the top half of a sheet of newsprint. Then have her rewrite it on the bottom half to show how a particular character's involvement impacts or changes the news story. Assemble the students' pages into a class newspaper; then place the paper at a reading center for any student to enjoy at her leisure.

Only Heroes Need Apply

Imagine the legends of American folklore pounding the pavement looking for other jobs! After students are familiar with the folk characters they've studied, have each student write a résumé for an assigned character using the reproducible form on page 37. Sort the completed résumés by job objective and then distribute them to cooperative groups. Ask the student groups to read each of the forms and decide on one applicant to hire. Have each group report to the class whom it hired and why.

Weather Folklore

Some people believe strongly in folk sayings or expressions related to the weather, such as:

- Flies swarm before a storm.
- A ring around the moon means rain is coming soon.
- The wider the brown band on the woolly-bear caterpillar, the milder the winter will be.

Ask your librarian to gather books about weather folklore such as those listed below for student groups to research. (Listings that are asterisked are out of print, but they may still be found in your school or public library.) Have each group list the weather sayings it finds and use them to write a humorous weather forecast for a cable television weather channel. Give all groups practice time before having them stand next to a national map and perform their forecasts for the class.

Suggested books:
And The Green Grass Grew All Around: Folk Poetry From Everyone by Alvin Schwartz (HarperCollins Children's Books, 1992)
*Animal Folklore: From Black Cats To White Horses by Edward F. Dolan (Ivy Books, 1992)
*Folklore Of American Weather by Eric Sloane (Duell, Sloan And Pearce, 1963)
*Nature's Weather Forecasters by Helen R. Sattler (Thomas Nelson Inc., Publishers; 1978)
Steven Caney's Kids' America (Workman Publishing Company, Inc.; 1978)
*The Old Farmer's Almanac: Book Of Weather Lore by Edward F. Dolan (Yankee Books, 1988)
*Weather Wisdom by Albert Lee (Doubleday & Company, Inc.; 1976)
Whoppers: Tall Tales And Other Lies Collected From American Folklore by Alvin Schwartz (HarperCollins Children's Books, 1990)

Legendary Endorsements

Imagine a towering image of John Henry endorsing a company's latest power tool or Stormalong advertising a new luxury yacht. Use images like these to review persuasive and clarification writing. Elicit from students examples of radio or TV commercials that use well-known athletes and celebrities to endorse products. Discuss with students the reasons companies hire these people to advertise their products. Ask if students have ever been persuaded to buy products because of their endorsors.

Next brainstorm with students a list of several different products to match with American legendary heroes and their traits. Then have each student choose a character/product combination. Ask the student to write a script for a commercial—focusing on the character's traits and known accomplishments—in which the character recommends the product to the public. Provide time for students to perform their commercials.

It's Debatable

Lots of debatable, science-related issues can be raised concerning the habits, occupations, or behaviors of some folklore characters. Should Paul Bunyan clear out forests, taking away animal homes and depleting natural resources in the process? Should men like John Henry lose their jobs when technology replaces humans with machines? Should Stormalong and his men introduce new whale-hunting techniques that will drastically decrease the whale population?

Ask students to help you add to this list of questions. Then make at least two copies of each question. Cut the questions apart and assign each one to a class member. Instruct the two students with the same question to research the pros and cons of their issue. After the allotted research time, have each student in the pair take one side of the issue to support. Then have each student translate the notes that support his side into a brief speech. On the debate day, ask students to be prepared to vote on the issue after hearing the opposing views presented by each pair. Appoint a student to tally the votes. Save the results to use in the "Graphed Dilemmas" activity that follows.

Graphed Dilemmas

Challenge students to turn the votes from the "It's Debatable" activity above into a variety of graphs. Provide each student with a copy of the voting results on each debated question, plus one sheet each of graph paper and unlined paper. Have the student use the data to produce two graphs: a line or bar graph on the graph paper; and a circle, picture, or stem-and-leaf graph on the unlined paper. Group and display the students' graphs on a bulletin board under enlarged copies of the debated questions.

Pro: Environmentalists everywhere will support Windwagon Smith's nonpolluting form of transportation.

Con: Windwagon Smith's prairie schooner would hurt the automobile industry and cause many workers to lose their jobs.

Puzzled No More

Have students create two-piece jigsaw puzzles to review the interesting tall tale or legendary folklore characters they learned about. Give each pupil a large white index card and ask her to pencil in a cutting line that divides it into two puzzle pieces. Assign each student a different folklore character. After cutting along the line of the card, have each student draw a picture of and label her character on one piece of the puzzle. Then, on the other piece, have the student write a description of the character and a list of the character's deeds. To make it a self-checking review, ask the student to write the character's initials on the backs of the two puzzle pieces. Place the completed puzzles in a review center for students to use during free time. Or for a fun way to pair students for a cooperative activity, randomly distribute the puzzle pieces; then have each pupil find her matching piece.

Big Books About Big Legends

As a culminating activity for your American folklore study, have the class create a big book. First have the class vote on its favorite character. Review with students all of the feats that this character accomplished. Together brainstorm other deeds the character did or incidents in which the character was involved. After recording all suggestions on the board, let the class vote on the deed or incident it wants to develop for the book. Keeping the sentences brief, write the story together from beginning to end. Have the students focus on using exaggeration and giving the character superhuman abilities.

When the story is complete, transfer it one sentence at a time onto numbered sheets of poster-board-sized chart paper. Based on the number of pages generated, give each individual or pair of students a page to illustrate. Place the completed pages between sheets of poster board decorated by the students. Bind the book along one side with metal rings. Then randomly select a committee of students to present the big book to a younger class.

Name _____ *Storytelling*

Tell Me A Story

Storytelling goes on almost every day in conversations with others. But some people have such a knack for telling stories that others can hardly wait to listen to them. Is there a secret to becoming a *storyteller* instead of just being a teller of stories?

Try these helpful hints and see what you think.

Hint #1:
Read several different folktales—tall tales, myths, or legends. Then select a tale that you think others will want to hear. If you choose a book that has illustrations, they will help you remember the characters and events more easily.

Hint #2:
Select a tale that is short—from two to five full pages—and that doesn't have to be told in rhyme.

Hint #3:
Find a quiet spot where you will not be disturbed. Read the tale three times.
- First read the tale to find out what happens—the *plot* (who has the problem, what the problem is, and how the problem is solved).
- Next read the tale to concentrate on the characters. Find out who each character is, what each one's relationship is to the other characters, how each one behaves and speaks, and what each one looks like.
- Finally read the tale to notice the order of the action. Be able to tell a little about each incident that happens.

Hint #4:
Close the book and tell the tale from beginning to end without stopping to look back. Don't worry if you leave out some details. Just concentrate on getting through the story one time.

Hint #5:
Reread the tale and find the parts you left out.

Hint #6:
Repeat steps 4 and 5 until you know the story well enough to tell it to an audience. Try tape-recording yourself; then play the tape back to listen for ways you can improve.

Additional Hints:
- Don't memorize the story word for word.
- Take a deep breath to relax before beginning to retell your folktale.
- Speak slowly and clearly.
- Personalize your tale with gestures, sound effects, a different dialect, or a disguised voice.
- Include a few similes or metaphors to help your audience be able to "see" what you describe.
  Example: He was as tall as the Empire State Building.
- Wear something a little special but not distracting.

©1996 The Education Center, Inc. • *DECEMBER* • TEC201

36   **Note To The Teacher:** Use these guidelines with "Tell Me A Story" on page 28. Duplicate a copy for each student.

Character development

Desperately Seeking Work

Your favorite folktale (or book) character is in need of a new job. Help this character find work quickly by filling in the necessary information on the résumé below. Then draw a flattering picture of the applicant inside the frame. Lots of other characters are applying for this job, too. So use your best effort to promote your character's qualities.

Objective (job desired): _____

_____

Previous work experience: _____

_____
_____
_____
_____
_____

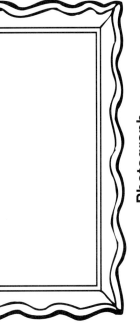

Name of character

References: _____

_____
_____

Photograph

Address: _____

Street number and name

_____
City   State

Education: _____

_____
_____

Reason(s) for leaving last job: _____

_____
_____
_____

©1996 The Education Center, Inc. • *DECEMBER* • TEC201

Bonus Box: Write a cover letter that your character can attach to the résumé. In the letter, have the character introduce himself/herself to the employer and tell briefly why he/she wants the job and would be a good employee.

Note To The Teacher: Use this reproducible with "Only Heroes Need Apply" on page 32 or as a book-report project after reading any book.

37

Name _____   *Problem solving*

Paul Bunyan's Breakfast

Ingmar, the lumberjack camp's new cook, has just finished making her first breakfast for Paul Bunyan. She listed the amount of each food item he ate so that she'd know how much to buy for future breakfasts. Use her note to help you work the following problems. Show your work on the back of this sheet.

Paul's Breakfast

3 dozen eggs
4 pounds of bacon
15 gallons of orange juice
30 gallons of milk
35 boxes of cornflakes
20 loaves of bread for toast
4 sticks of butter

1. How many individual eggs does Paul eat for breakfast each morning? _____

2. If Ingmar has a five-day supply of cornflakes, how many boxes does she have? _____

3. If four sticks of butter are used to butter all 20 loaves of bread for toast, how many loaves can be buttered with just one stick of butter? _____

4. Since one pound equals 16 ounces, how many ounces of bacon does Paul eat? _____

5. If bacon costs $6.00 per pound, how much would Ingmar spend just on bacon for Paul's breakfast? _____

6. If milk is $1.69 a gallon at one store and $1.79 a gallon at another store, how much will Ingmar save if she buys Paul's 30 gallons at the lower price? _____

7. Since one gallon equals four quarts, how many quarts of milk does Paul drink at his first meal of the day? _____

8. How many more quarts of milk than quarts of orange juice does Paul drink at breakfast? _____

9. Because it's on sale, Ingmar wants to buy a week's supply of butter for Paul. How many sticks will she need to buy? _____

10. If a loaf of bread is on sale at two loaves for $1.00, how much will Ingmar pay for one day's supply of Paul's breakfast bread? _____

Bonus Box: On the back of this sheet, list the amount and types of foods that Paul Bunyan would eat for lunch.

Patterns
Use with "Tracking American Folklore" on page 30.

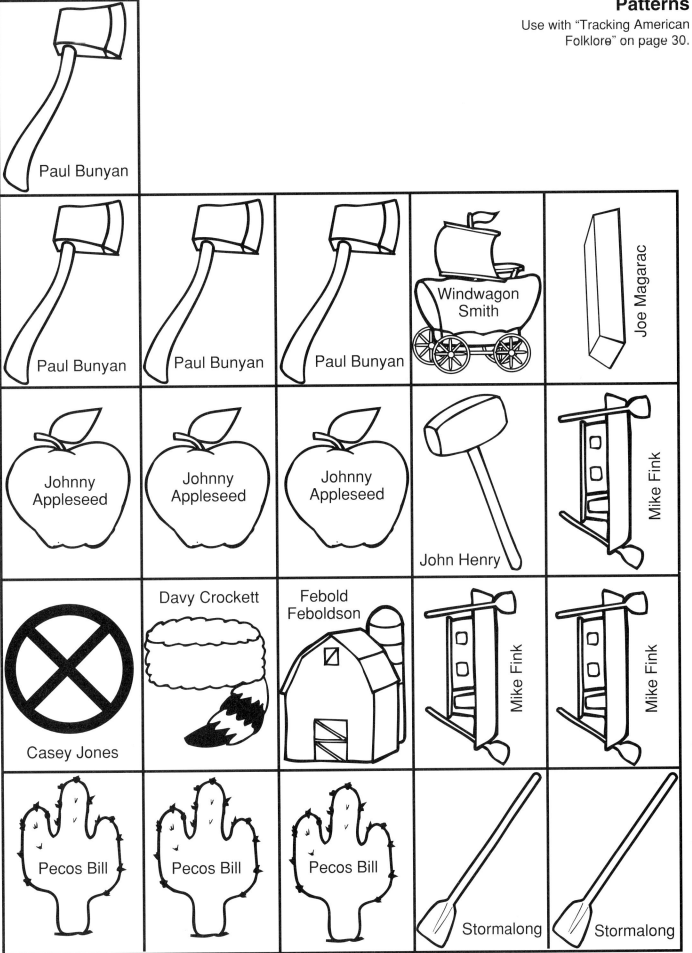

Eight Nights, Eight Lights
Sharing The Rich Tradition Of Hanukkah

Hanukkah is one of the happiest of times for Jewish families. This eight-day holiday—also called the Festival Of Lights—includes games, songs, stories, gifts, and the lighting of a special candelabra called the *menorah*. Bring this 2,400-year-old tradition into your classroom with the following creative teaching suggestions.

by Paula Holdren

A Brief History Of Hanukkah

When Jewish families gather to celebrate Hanukkah, they commemorate a time more than 2,000 years ago when their ancestors were forbidden to observe the Sabbath. The city of Jerusalem and the Jews' beloved temple were taken over by the Syrians, and many holy items were broken or destroyed. Judah Maccabee and a small group of Jewish farmers rebelled against the Syrians and reclaimed the city and temple. The temple was reconsecrated in a celebration that lasted eight days. Judah decreed that the anniversary of the reconsecration should be celebrated for eight days every year. After cleaning the temple, Judah's companions searched for oil to relight the Eternal Light. There was barely enough oil to last one day. It was lit anyway and miraculously the oil lasted for eight days until new oil arrived. Hanukkah lasts for eight days and reminds Jewish people of this miracle and their ancestors' successful fight for religious freedom.

A Window On Hanukkah

Happiness—with generous doses of fun and games mixed in—best describes Hanukkah. To highlight this special time, decorate a bulletin board to resemble a large, eight-paned window. Use blue paper (representing justice), white borders and windowpane dividers (representing truth), and gold lettering (representing the lamp of Eternal Light). Divide students into eight groups. Assign each group one windowpane of the board. Instruct each group to fill its pane with an item, symbol, or picture that represents the spirit of Hanukkah.

A Window On Hanukkah

In Our Own Words

More than likely, many of your students may not know the whos, whats, and whys of Hanukkah. Provide them with an even better understanding by inviting a rabbi or other Jewish citizen of your community to your classroom to share the story of Hanukkah. Ask the visitor(s) to bring personal items, such as menorahs and dreidels, and to recall family traditions that he or she treasures most. Make sure that students have the opportunity to ask lots of questions.

Out Of The Darkness

A menorah is a special type of candelabra with eight candleholders—one for each night of the festival that commemorates the miracle of the sacred oil. A central *shammesh,* or helper candle, is used to light the others. After darkness falls, families gather to light the candles—one the first night, two the second night, and so on until all of the candles are lit.

Times have changed and so have menorahs. In addition to the popular traditional shape, menorahs in various interesting and unique designs are now available. A menorah simply must have eight candleholders plus space for a shammesh which should be elevated above the others. After viewing traditional menorahs (or pictures), review the two requirements mentioned above. Challenge your students' creativity by having them draw and/or build "new" menorahs. Then brainstorm interesting themes and media to use. Menorahs can take any shape and can be made of any materials. They can be large or small. But most all, they're fun to create!

Easy Menorahs: These paper-plate menorahs will stand tall during the Hanukkah season, or you can attach them to a bulletin board to complement seasonal creative writings.
1. Fold a paper plate in half to serve as the base.
2. Cut four straws in half for candles. Glue or tape four on either side of the plate.
3. Cut one straw a little longer than the rest and secure it in the center as a shammesh.
4. Crumple orange tissue paper into small tufts to represent flames. Stuff the tissue into the top of each straw.

Oil Lamp Menorahs: These bright menorahs make great table centerpieces.
1. Pour olive oil into eight small glass containers, such as baby-food jars.
2. Cut eight 2 1/2-inch lengths of wick.
3. Submerge a wick in each container of oil, leaving about 1/4 inch of wick above the surface.
4. Arrange four containers on either side of a candle (shammesh).

Delightful Dreidels

Jewish people were not allowed to pray or study under Syrian rule. When they secretly gathered to study and pray, they brought along small tops called *dreidels* and began to play with them when soldiers were around. In doing so, they could escape potential punishment.

A dreidel is a four-sided object with a Hebrew letter on each side. The letters are the first letters of the Hebrew words that mean "a great miracle happened there." Have your students follow the directions below to make their own dreidels. Provide each student with a copy of the dreidel game rules on page 44, which also includes the letters needed to complete the dreidel.

Egg-Carton Dreidels: Cut off two sections of a cardboard egg carton. Paint both sections. When the paint has dried, tape the open ends together. Cut out the Hebrew letters on page 44 and glue one to each side of the dreidel. Stick a sharpened pencil through the dreidel.

Paper Dreidels: Mark and cut a 3-inch square from an index card. Draw diagonals on the square. Cut out the Hebrew letters on page 44 and glue one in each section of the square. Push a sharp-pointed toothpick through the center of the card at the intersection of the two diagonals.

The Best Gift

Friendship, kindness, love, and loyalty are gifts that reflect the true spirit of Hanukkah gift-giving. These priceless gifts are available to anyone at no cost! Yet their value is immeasurable. Brainstorm with your class to determine a "student-to-student" gift wish list—gifts that don't cost money. Items might include eating lunch together, helping with a particular subject area, sharing a good book, helping clean a desk, or completing a classroom job together. Next have students write their names on slips of paper and place them in a hat. Have each student then draw a name for a class gift exchange.

Instruct each student to determine the gift he will give his classmate. Provide each student with a brightly colored piece of paper and a length of ribbon. Have the student describe his gift on the piece of paper, roll it up like a scroll, then tie it with the ribbon. Invite students to exchange gifts, filling the eight days of Hanukkah with goodwill and caring for one another.

Tell Me The Story Of Hanukkah

Hanukkah may be a holiday that is unfamiliar to many students. To spread the news about this special holiday, check to see if your class can be responsible for leading oral-reading storytimes for several primary classes during their library periods. With assistance from your media specialist, select several Hanukkah books and assign them to individuals or small groups in your class (see the list of books on page 44). Have each student (or group) familiarize himself with the book so that he will feel comfortable reading it aloud to younger students. Vary the participants, stories, and schedule so that everyone has the opportunity to share a story of Hanukkah with the younger children. Or team up with one primary-grades teacher and plan story-sharing sessions during the eight days of Hanukkah.

Love Those Latkes!

What would Hanukkah be without latkes? These yummy potato pancakes are a holiday food tradition that Jewish families enjoy as a much-anticipated part of their celebrations. Latkes are eaten because they are prepared in oil, a symbol of Hanukkah.

Invite parent volunteers to come to class with their electric skillets and spatulas. Organize the necessary supplies so that small groups of students divide up the responsibilities—and fun!—of cooking and eating these tasty treats.

Potato Latkes

Ingredients:
4 potatoes
2 eggs (beaten)
1 teaspoon salt
3 tablespoons flour
1/2 teaspoon grated onion
oil for frying

Directions:
1. Peel the potatoes and grate them finely. Squeeze them dry.
2. Add the onion, beaten eggs, flour, and salt.
3. Stir until well blended.
4. Drop the batter by tablespoonfuls into hot oil.
5. Fry until both sides are crisp and brown.
6. Drain on paper towels and serve hot with applesauce or sour cream.

Linking Up With Literature

Be sure to share some of the following outstanding literature with your students during the Hanukkah season:

- *The Hanukkah Ghosts* by Malka Penn (Holiday House, Inc.; 1995)
- *The Gift* by Aliana Brodmann (Simon & Schuster, 1993)
- *Spotted Pony: A Collection Of Hanukkah Stories* retold by Eric A. Kimmel (Holiday House, Inc; 1992)
- *Hanukkah Lights, Hanukkah Nights* by Leslie Kimmelman (HarperCollins Children's Books, 1992)
- *The Story Of Hanukkah* by Bobbi Katz (Random House Books For Young Readers, 1995)

Let's Play The Dreidel Game!

Nun
(Do nothing.)

Gimel
(Take all of the pot.)

He
(Take half of the pot.)

Shin
(Put two items in the pot.)

Directions:
1. Divide the playing pieces (beans, hard candies, buttons, peanuts, etc.) equally among all players.
2. Each player places one item in the center of the playing area—the "pot."
3. The first player spins the dreidel and follows the direction that matches his spin.
4. Play then continues to the left.
5. Play continues until each player has had a certain number of spins or the game has been played for a predetermined length of time.
6. When there are no items in the pot, repeat step 2.
7. The winner is the player with the most items at the end of the game.

Math Hint: When you take half of the pot—and the pot has an odd number of items—round up the number. For example: 1/2 of 7 = 3 1/2 = **4**; 1/2 of 11 = 5 1/2 = **6**; etc.

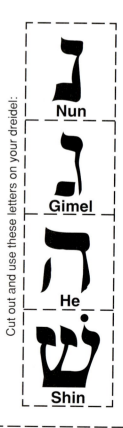

Cut out and use these letters on your dreidel:

©1996 The Education Center, Inc. • DECEMBER • TEC201

Note To The Teacher: Use this reproducible with "Delightful Dreidels" on page 42. Provide each group of students with a supply of items such as those listed in Step 1 to use as playing pieces.

Name_____   Geometry

The Star Of David

The six-pointed Star of David is also called *Magen David,* which means "Shield of David." It was believed to have been a decoration on King David's shield. For hundreds of years it was used by Jews as well as non-Jews. In the 19th century, the Star of David began to appear in synagogue decorations. It became a symbol of the Jews. It now appears on the flag of the State of Israel, as well as on Jewish religious objects.

Take a closer look at this star—a truly unique geometric shape! Complete each fact below with a geometry word, one letter per blank. One letter is already included for you. Happy Hanukkah!

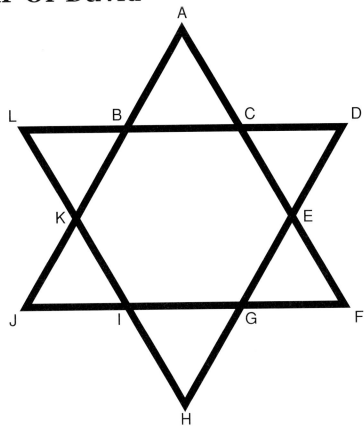

1. This six-pointed star is called a **H** __ __ __ __ __ __.
2. Its measure is less than 90°, so angle GHI is an **A** __ __ __ __ angle.
3. Shape BDGJ is a **P** __ __ __ __ __ __ __ __ __ __ __.
4. A hexagon is a six-sided **P** __ __ __ __ __ __.
5. Angles ACD and ACB are __ __ __ __ __ __ __ __ __ __ __ __ __ __ __ __ **Y** angles. Their measures total 180°.
6. Shape BDGJ, with its four equal sides, is also a __ **H** __ __ __ __ __ __.
7. Draw a segment from points K to E. Shape BCEK is a __ __ **A** __ __ __ __ __ __.
8. Segments LD and AF __ **N** __ __ __ __ __ __ __ at point C.
9. Triangle AFJ is __ __ __ __ __ **U** __ __ __ to triangle LDH.
10. Look at shape BCEGIK. Segment **K** __ is one of its lines of symmetry.
11. Triangle LDH is similar to triangle __ __ **K**. They have the same shape.
12. Triangle ABC is an __ __ __ __ __ __ **A** __ __ __ __ __ triangle.
13. Shape BCEGIK is a **H** __ __ __ __ __ __ __.

Bonus Box: Suppose segment AB is three inches long. What is the perimeter of the star?

©1996 The Education Center, Inc. • *DECEMBER* • TEC201 • Key p. 95

45

Let Freedom Ring!
Activities To Celebrate America's Freedoms

Why are we Americans so patriotic? Perhaps it's the memory of how our relatives and ancestors struggled to gain and preserve our country's freedoms. On December 15 we celebrate an important date in the history of freedom—the signing of the Bill of Rights. Use the following activities to examine the events and issues of freedom.

by Beth Gress

More Than A Definition

What is freedom? Does freedom mean being able to do whatever you want? How does your freedom affect another person's freedom? Discuss each of these questions with your class. Then have each student write a definition of freedom in his journal. Next divide the class into six groups. Give each group a dictionary and one of the definitions of freedom written below. Instruct each group to rewrite the definition in its own words. Then challenge each group to design a skit to illustrate its definition of freedom. After each group shares its skit, instruct each student to revisit his original definition of freedom to see if his understanding has changed.

- condition of being free of restraints
- liberty from slavery, detention, or oppression
- political independence
- immunity from the arbitrary exercise of authority
- the capacity to exercise choice; free will
- the right of enjoying all of the privileges of membership or citizenship

Reflections Of Freedom

"Proclaim Liberty throughout all the land unto all the inhabitants thereof," reads the inscription on the Liberty Bell. This bell tolled on July 8, 1776, to announce the adoption of the Declaration of Independence. Can your students imagine what it would be like to give their lives for the cause of freedom? After completing "More Than A Definition" on page 46, instruct each student to write a paragraph about freedom using one of the following topics:

- What Freedom Means To Me
- My Most Important Freedom
- Freedom: A Privilege
- Freedom = New Responsibilities
- Freedom is different now than _____ because…
- The most important fight for freedom was _____ because…

Duplicate the Liberty Bell pattern on page 54 for each student. Instruct the student to cut out the bell shape and copy her paragraph onto it. Then have her make a cover by tracing the bell onto a piece of gold or brown paper. After adding realistic details to the cover, have the student attach it on top of the paragraph by stapling them together at the top only. Finally staple the top of each bell to a bulletin board under the title "Let Freedom Ring!"

Lady Liberty

People around the world view the Statue of Liberty as a symbol of freedom. On its pedestal is a plaque inscribed with a poem titled "The New Colossus." The poem, written by Emma Lazarus, closes with the following famous lines:

Give me your tired, your poor,
Your huddled masses yearning to breathe free,
The wretched refuse of your teeming shore.
Send these, the homeless, tempest-tost, to me.
I lift my lamp beside the golden door!

Discuss the meaning of these lines with your students. Explain that this landmark, technically titled "Liberty Enlightening The World," has been the welcoming beacon to immigrants sailing to the United States via New York harbor for more than 100 years. Enlarge the Lady Liberty pattern on page 55. Post it on a wall or bulletin board. Then ask students to think about what Lady Liberty would have to say about the way that Americans use or misuse their freedoms or the freedoms of others. Give each student a large, white sheet of paper to cut into the shape of a speech balloon. After writing an imaginary quote by Lady Liberty on her speech balloon, have each student place her balloon around the picture of Lady Liberty.

Rights/Freedoms	Responsibilities
Getting Married	Need a job to support a family.
	Must pay the bills.
	Need to spend time with family members.
Driving A Car	Must drive responsibly.
	Must have license and car insurance.
	Must keep the car in good repair.

Kids Have Rights, Too

Theoretically all Americans are free. However, children observe that adults have far more freedoms and rights than they do. As a class brainstorm a list of rights that children do not share with adults, such as those from the list at the left. Next divide students into groups to discuss reasons why kids should or should not be granted these rights. Remind students that with every new freedom comes a new responsibility. Have each group make two columns on a sheet of paper. On one side, instruct the groups to list freedoms that adults do not share with children. On the opposite column, have each group list one or more responsibilities that go with each freedom.

For homework, have each student interview two or three adults to find out if they agree that it's fair that children don't have these rights. Instruct students to ask for reasons and take notes during the interviews. In class compare the answers given by parents with the thoughts shared by students the previous day.

Constitutional Quiz Show

There's nothing like a classroom game show to help you review important facts. Duplicate the questions on page 56 and cut them apart. Tape each question onto an index card. On the opposite side of the card, write the point value for that question. Tape the cards on the chalkboard as shown.

Divide the class into groups of four or five students. Give each group a small chalkboard on which to record its answers. Read the names of the categories aloud for the students and remind them that the higher the point value, the harder the question. Instruct a member from the starting team to select a category and point value. Read the question aloud. Then give the team 30 seconds to agree on an answer. If the answer is correct, reward that team with the given points. If the answer is incorrect, allow the other teams to answer the question. Instruct those teams to decide on an answer and then write it on their boards. At your signal, have all the teams hold up their boards. Each team with a correct answer earns the points for that question. Continue the game with the next team. Proclaim the team with the highest points the winner.

Historical Timeline

Since the late 1700s, many events have led to and reinforced the freedoms that Americans enjoy. Help students explore these historical milestones by duplicating the pattern on page 55. Assign each student one of the events listed below. Instruct each student to conduct research on that event and complete the pattern; then have each child color his pattern. Display the completed patterns along a wall in chronological order. Have each student report on his event by sharing the most significant thing he learned while researching.

April 19, 1775: The American Revolution begins with the battles of Lexington and Concord.
July 4, 1776: The Declaration of Independence is signed.
March 1, 1781: The Articles of Confederation go into effect.
October 19, 1781: British General Cornwallis surrenders at Yorktown.
April 19, 1783: The Confederation Congress declares an official end to the Revolutionary War.
August 1786: Shay's Rebellion in Massachusetts shows the weakness of the national government.
February 21, 1787: The Confederation Congress calls for a Constitutional Convention.
September 17, 1787: The Constitution is signed by 39 men from the 12 states represented at the Convention.
June 21, 1788: The Constitution goes into effect with the approval of the ninth state, New Hampshire.
April 30, 1789: George Washington is sworn in as the first president under the Constitution.
July 16, 1790: Legislation is signed making the District of Columbia the permanent federal capital, beginning in 1800.
December 15, 1791: Virginia is the 11th state to ratify ten of the proposed amendments. They become the first ten amendments to the Constitution—the Bill of Rights.
December 6, 1865: Slavery is abolished with the ratification of the Thirteenth Amendment.
July 9, 1868: Emancipated slaves are guaranteed citizenship, suffrage, and due process by the Fourteenth Amendment.
February 3, 1870: Former male slaves are guaranteed the right to vote by the Fifteenth Amendment.
August 18, 1920: Women are granted the right to vote by the Nineteenth Amendment.
1964: The Civil Rights Act of 1964 is passed, banning discrimination due to a person's color, race, national origin, religion, or sex.
January 23, 1964: The Twenty-fourth Amendment is ratified, allowing people to vote without paying a tax.
July 1, 1971: All citizens 18 years or older can vote with the ratification of the Twenty-sixth Amendment.
1988: The Civil Liberties Act of 1988 gave Japanese Americans who were unjustly interned during World War II an apology and money from the U.S. government.

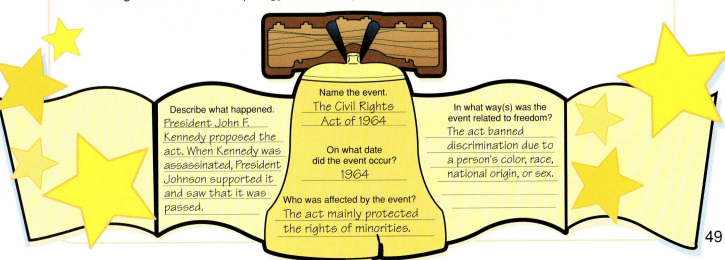

Postage Stamp Of Approval

Many of our U.S. postage stamps depict topics dealing with government and freedom. Invite students to help you collect canceled postage stamps that have a historical theme. Then instruct each student to design a new postage stamp that commemorates one of the amendments in the Bill of Rights. Duplicate a copy of the Bill of Rights on page 58 for each student. Divide the class into ten groups. Assign one of the ten amendments to each group. Have each group reread the amendment and summarize its meaning on a sheet of paper. Under the summary, have the group list situations that could be illustrated to depict that right. Provide each group with a 12" x 18" sheet of light-colored paper. Then have the group select one of the situations to illustrate as an oversized postage stamp. After illustrating the event, have each group trim around the edge of the paper with pinking shears to create a giant stamp. Post these stamps on a hallway wall under the title "These Rights Have Our Stamp Of Approval!"

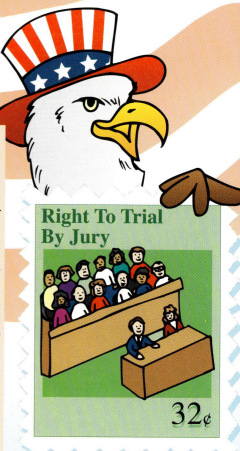

A New Amendment

Once students have become familiar with the rights protected under our Constitution and Bill of Rights, follow up by asking them, "Are there any rights that are being neglected in our country today? Are there injustices that need to be set straight?" Begin by brainstorming some of the problems that face our country. Divide the class into small groups and assign to each group one of the problems you've listed on the board. Have each group brainstorm solutions to the problem; then allow each group to share its problem and list of solutions. Next duplicate the pattern on page 59 on yellow paper for each group. Instruct each group to write a formal sentence stating the problem on the lines beginning with "Whereas…." Then, on the lines following "We hereby propose…," have each group write a formal amendment that presents one or more of the group's solutions to its problem. Number the patterns; then post them on a large sheet of red bulletin-board paper under the title "New Amendments For America."

Spread The Word

Spread the word about U.S. rights by participating in this simple community outreach activity. Obtain a supply of donated paper grocery bags from a local supermarket. Make sure that the bags have at least one blank side. Give each student one to three bags to decorate. Instruct the student to illustrate a symbol of freedom or one of the rights from our Constitution on the bag. Then have her add a caption explaining the illustration. Gather up the completed bags and return them to the store to be used for packing groceries.

The 19th Amendment gave women the right to vote.

It's Only Naturalization!

America is known around the world as being the "land of the free," making it an attractive place to immigrate. However, in order to qualify for U.S. citizenship, or *naturalization*, each foreign applicant must meet the following requirements (the procedures may vary for children of foreign nationals, war veterans, spouses of U.S. citizens, and permanent residents over the age of 50):

- Lawful admission as a resident
- Continuous residence for five years before filing for naturalization
- Residence for at least three months in the state where the application is filed
- Physical presence within the United States for at least one-half of the period required for continuous residence
- Good moral character
- Continuous residence in the United States from the date of filing to the date of the oath of citizenship
- Age 18 or older at the time of filing
- Ability to read, write, and speak English
- Knowledge of U.S. history and government

Once they've completed the naturalization process, applicants pledge an oath of allegiance to the United States during a citizenship ceremony.

Discuss the above citizenship requirements with your students. Have students write some questions that they think applicants for U.S. citizenship should be able to answer in order to become U.S. citizens. Make up a sample citizenship test using questions contributed by the students. Then have each student take the sample test.

For more information on the process of naturalization, search the Internet using the keyword *naturalization* or write to the Office of Information, Immigration and Naturalization Service, Department of Justice, 425 I St. NW, Washington, DC 20536.

Bill Of Rights Day

Don't forget to celebrate Bill of Rights Day on December 15. Integrate some of the following activities into your celebration:

- Begin the day with a color-guard ceremony. Have selected students raise the school flag. Then lead the class in several patriotic songs.
- Invite students to wear red, white, and blue clothing to school that day.
- Have a few students read their freedom reports (see "Let Freedom Ring" on page 47) over the loudspeaker during the morning announcements.
- Have several students dress up as historical figures and position themselves in the hallway. As younger students pass by, have the historical figures introduce themselves and give a little information about why they are famous.
- Play the Constitutional Quiz Show game described on page 48.
- Schedule a field trip to a state capitol, city hall, courthouse, or jail.
- Set aside a space in the cafeteria. During lunchtime, have students perform skits portraying events in our country's struggle for freedom.

Hard At Work

The delegates to the Constitutional Convention spent several months writing the Constitution and the Bill of Rights. Read aloud the book *Shh! We're Writing The Constitution* by Jean Fritz (Putnam Publishing Group) or *If You Were There When They Signed The Constitution* by Elizabeth Levy (Scholastic Inc.). As each student listens to the story, have him write down important quotes or opinions that each of the main characters presented. Have each student choose one of the quotes to write in a speech bubble cut from white paper. Then have him draw, cut out, and label an illustration of the person who spoke the quotes. Post the pictures and the speech bubbles down a hallway wall under the title "Insights From An Infant Nation."

To Be Cherished

Citizens of the United States have so many freedoms that it's easy to take these privileges for granted. Give your students a new perspective on the freedoms they enjoy by comparing current events from the United States and other countries. Divide a bulletin board into two sections. Label one side of the board "Freedoms We Enjoy." Instruct students to bring in and post news articles that relate to freedoms guaranteed by the Bill of Rights or other Constitutional amendments (for instance, an article about gun control). Label the other side of the bulletin board "Striving For Freedom." On this side of the board, have students place articles about situations that reflect the lack of freedom in other countries around the world, such as the conflict in Bosnia. As a student posts an article, have her share a summary of it and her opinion on the article's topic.

Freedom Fighters

The words of the Constitution guaranteed the rights of American citizens. However, its framers overlooked several groups of Americans, including women, African Americans (both slave and free), Native Americans, and the poor. Over the years leaders stepped forward to devote their time and energy to the cause of freedom for *all* American citizens. Have each student research one of the freedom fighters listed below. Duplicate the pattern and directions for making a booklet on page 59 for each student. After the student constructs the booklet, have him research and illustrate the following information:

Page 1: Record the person's birth and death dates, the place of birth, and any interesting childhood experiences.
Page 2: Describe the person's career, marriage, and any other information about his or her adulthood.
Page 3: Summarize how this person helped the cause of freedom.

Jane Addams
Marian Anderson
Susan B. Anthony
Mary McLeod Bethune
Margaret Bourke-White
John Brown
Carrie Chapman Catt
Chief Joseph

Frederick Douglass
W. E. B. Du Bois
Betty Friedan
Geronimo
Langston Hughes
Jesse Jackson
Lyndon B. Johnson
Martin Luther King, Jr.

Abraham Lincoln
Malcolm X
Lucretia Mott
Sandra Day O'Connor
Ely Samuel Parker
Rosa Lee Parks
Eleanor Roosevelt
Margaret Sanger

Sitting Bull
Elizabeth Cady Stanton
Lucy Stone
Sojourner Truth
Harriet Tubman
Booker T. Washington
Woodrow Wilson
Victoria Woodhull

Pattern
Use with "Reflections Of Freedom" on page 47.

Name
©1996 The Education Center, Inc. • *DECEMBER* • TEC201

Patterns
Use with "Lady Liberty" on page 47.

©1996 The Education Center, Inc. • DECEMBER • TEC201

Use with "Historical Timeline" on page 49.

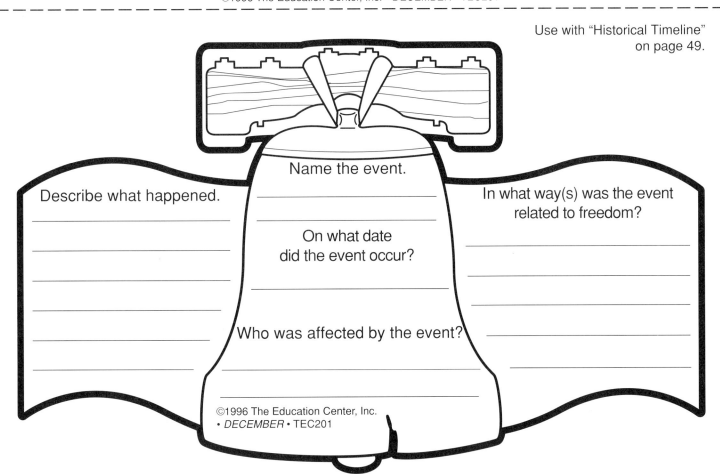

55

Amendments And The Bill Of Rights	Freedom Symbols	Our Government	Historical Figures	Constitutional Convention
10 **Q.** Which amendment to the Constitution guarantees freedom of the press, freedom of speech, and freedom of religion? **A.** The First Amendment	**10** **Q.** What country presented the Statue of Liberty to the United States as a gift? **A.** France	**10** **Q.** How many senators from each state are in Congress? **A.** Two	**10** **Q.** Which president issued the Emancipation Proclamation in 1863 declaring freedom for all slaves? **A.** Abraham Lincoln	**10** **Q.** What general was elected president of the Constitutional Convention? **A.** George Washington
20 **Q.** How many amendments to the Constitution make up the Bill of Rights? **A.** Ten	**20** **Q.** What city is the home of the Liberty Bell? **A.** Philadelphia	**20** **Q.** What are the names of the two parts of Congress? **A.** The Senate and The House of Representatives	**20** **Q.** Who wrote the Declaration of Independence? **A.** Thomas Jefferson	**20** **Q.** In what city was the Constitutional Convention held? **A.** Philadelphia
30 **Q.** The Eighteenth Amendment made the sale of a product illegal. The Twenty-first Amendment made it legal again. What was the product? **A.** Alcohol	**30** **Q.** What animal is shown on the Seal of the United States of America? **A.** The eagle	**30** **Q.** What are the three branches of the government? **A.** executive, legislative, and judicial	**30** **Q.** What black preacher fought for equal rights for blacks and gave the famous "I Have A Dream" speech? **A.** Martin Luther King, Jr.	**30** **Q.** Which delegate never missed a day and recorded notes during every session of the Constitutional Convention? **A.** James Madison
40 **Q.** How many amendments to the Constitution are there? **A.** 26	**40** **Q.** What two words were officially added to the Pledge of Allegiance more than 50 years after the pledge was written? **A.** "under God"	**40** **Q.** What is the name given to the group of advisors that the president appoints to head various departments of the government? **A.** The cabinet	**40** **Q.** Which patriot said the famous line, "Give me liberty or give me death"? **A.** Patrick Henry	**40** **Q.** In what year was the Constitutional Convention held? **A.** 1787
50 **Q.** Where are the Constitution and the Bill of Rights on display for the public? **A.** The National Archives in Washington, D.C.	**50** **Q.** What American symbol has a song about it written by Francis Scott Key? **A.** The flag (The song was "The Star-Spangled Banner.")	**50** **Q.** How many justices serve on the Supreme Court? **A.** Nine	**50** **Q.** What woman, pictured on a $1 coin, was important in the fight for women's right to vote? **A.** Susan B. Anthony	**50** **Q.** What was the name of the plan that created the three branches of government as outlined in the Constitution? **A.** The Virginia Plan

©1996 The Education Center, Inc. • *DECEMBER* • TEC201

Note To The Teacher: Use this page with "Constitutional Quiz Show" on page 48.

Name _____   *The Constitutional Amendments*

How Well Do You Know Your Rights?

Each statement on the grid below is based on one of the amendments to the Constitution. Some of the statements are true and others are false. Read each statement. Write a **+** in the circle if the statement is true and a **0** in the circle if the statement is false. Then decide which amendment is being addressed in each statement. Write the number of the amendment on the line under each statement.

We The People...

○ **T**	○ **C**	○ **I**	○ **M**
1. You may be charged a fee in order to vote.	2. The police may come inside your home at any time to conduct a search.	3. Women can vote.	4. You may have a lawyer defend you in a trial, even if you can't afford one.
Amendment # ___	Amendment # ___	Amendment # ___	Amendment # ___
○ **E**	○ **E**	○ **S**	○ **E**
5. A judge can send you to jail without a trial if he is sure you are guilty.	6. Slavery is no longer legal.	7. You have to be at least 18 years old to vote.	8. You cannot own a gun unless you have served in the military.
Amendment # ___	Amendment # ___	Amendment # ___	Amendment # ___
○ **A**	○ **B**	○ **N**	○ **D**
9. You do not have to testify if you are the one on trial.	10. Newspapers can print opinions about government even if the opinions are critical.	11. People who live in the District of Columbia cannot vote for president.	12. All alcohol sales are illegal.
Amendment # ___	Amendment # ___	Amendment # ___	Amendment # ___
○ **S**	○ **E**	○ **P**	○ **R**
13. The federal government may collect income taxes.	14. A President may serve for 12 years.	15. Police can treat you cruelly if you are found guilty of a crime.	16. You are entitled to rights other than those listed in the Constitution.
Amendment # ___	Amendment # ___	Amendment # ___	Amendment # ___

Of all the delegates, only George Washington and James Madison had something special in common. What was it? To find out, cut apart the 16 boxes. Arrange them in order of the amendments. The letters in the upper right-hand corner of each grid will spell out the answer.

©1996 The Education Center, Inc. • *DECEMBER* • TEC201 • Key p. 95

Note To The Teacher: Use this page to pretest your students' knowledge of the Constitution. Or provide each student with a copy of the Constitution. Then have him research each statement in order to familiarize himself with the amendments.

Name _____   Bill of Rights, vocabulary

The United States Bill Of Rights

Did you know that the writers of the Constitution did not originally plan to include a Bill of Rights? They felt that these rights were understood and did not need to be spelled out. However, today many controversies center around these very rights! Read each of the following Bill of Rights amendments. On another piece of paper, work with your group to rewrite the main points of each amendment in your own words. Use a dictionary to help you.

The Amendments

1. Congress shall make no law respecting an establishment of religion, or prohibiting the free exercise thereof; or abridging the freedom of speech, or of the press; or the right of the people peaceably to assemble, and to petition the government for a redress of grievances.

2. A well-regulated militia being necessary to the security of a free State, the right of the people to keep and bear arms shall not be infringed.

3. No soldier shall, in time of peace, be quartered in any house without the consent of the owner; nor in time of war but in a manner to be prescribed by law.

4. The right of the people to be secure in their persons, houses, papers and effects, against unreasonable searches and seizures, shall not be violated, and no warrants shall issue but upon probable cause, supported by oath or affirmation, and particularly describing the place to be searched, and the persons or things to be seized.

5. No person shall be held to answer for a capital or otherwise infamous crime, unless on a presentment or indictment of a grand jury, except in cases arising in the land or naval forces, or in the militia, when in actual service in time of war or public danger; nor shall any person be subject for the same offense to be twice put in jeopardy of life or limb; nor shall be compelled in any criminal case to be a witness against himself, nor be deprived of life, liberty, or property, without due process of law; nor shall private property be taken for public use, without just compensation.

6. In all criminal prosecutions the accused shall enjoy the right to a speedy and public trial, by an impartial jury of the State and district wherein the crime shall have been committed, which district shall have been previously ascertained by law, and to be informed of the nature and cause of the accusation; to be confronted with the witnesses against him; to have compulsory process for obtaining witnesses in his favor, and to have the assistance of counsel for his defense.

7. In suits at common law, where the value in controversy shall exceed twenty dollars, the right of trial by jury shall be preserved, and no fact tried by a jury shall be otherwise reexamined in any court of the United States than according to the rules of the common law.

8. Excessive bail shall not be required, nor excessive fines imposed, nor cruel and unusual punishments inflicted.

9. The enumeration in the Constitution of certain rights shall not be construed to deny or disparage others retained by the people.

10. The powers not delegated to the United States by the Constitution, nor prohibited by it to the States, are reserved to the States respectively, or to the people.

©1996 The Education Center, Inc. • *DECEMBER* • TEC201 • Key p. 95

Note To The Teacher: Use this page with "Postage Stamp Of Approval" on page 50 and "Bill Of Rights Day" on page 52. The answer key is on page 95.

Patterns
Use with "A New Amendment" on page 50.

Amendment # _____

Whereas _____
_____
_____
_____

We hereby propose _____
_____
_____
_____
_____

Signed _____
_____

©1996 The Education Center, Inc. • DECEMBER • TEC201

Name Of Freedom Fighter

by

Name Of Student

©1996 The Education Center, Inc. • DECEMBER • TEC201

Use with "Freedom Fighters" on page 53.

Directions:
1. Get three 8 1/2" x 5 1/2" sheets of paper and a pair of scissors.
2. Measure and cut a one-inch strip from the short end of one sheet of paper; measure and cut a two-inch strip from the short end of another sheet.
3. Cut out, color, and label this cover page.
4. Stack the papers and line up the left margins as shown. Staple.
5. Complete your report following your teacher's directions.

Note To The Teacher: Provide each student with three 8 1/2" x 5 1/2" sheets of paper, scissors, markers or crayons, a stapler, and a ruler.

A Winter Wonderland
Thematic Activities For Frosty Winter Days

Winter—the coldest season of the year—comes to the Northern Hemisphere in December and lasts until late March. During this period, the hemisphere is tilted farthest away from the sun. The Southern Hemisphere experiences its winter season six months later—from about June 20 until late September. Warm up even the frostiest winter days with these terrific cross-curricular activities!

by Peggy W. Hambright

The Coldest Solstice

Zero in on the scientific reason for the season by sharing the winter portion of Gail Gibbons's book *The Reasons For Seasons* (Holiday House, Inc.) with your students. Help them understand why it's cold in winter by having each student make the winter solstice model below. After making the model, give each student an enlarged copy of the polar-bear pattern on page 67. On his pattern, have the student write a paragraph that explains why the earth's Northern and Southern Hemispheres do not experience winter at the same time. Attach the polar-bear paragraphs to the models and display them in the room.

Materials for each student:
- one 9" x 12" sheet of black construction paper
- 1/2 of a tennis-ball-sized sphere of Styrofoam®
- one golf-ball-sized sphere of Styrofoam®, cut in half
- green, blue, black, and yellow paint (watercolor or tempera)
- small paintbrush
- small cup of water
- two crayons—one yellow and one white
- one foot of colorful yarn, cut in two six-inch lengths
- glue

Steps for each student:
1. Paint the tennis-ball-sized Styrofoam® hemisphere yellow. Use black paint to label it "Sun" and glue it in the center of the black paper.
2. Paint each of the two golf-ball-sized Styrofoam® hemispheres to look like the earth's Western Hemisphere—making the continents green and the oceans blue.
3. Paint the equator on each Western Hemisphere with black paint.
4. Glue the two Western Hemispheric halves on the black paper to the left and right of the sun.
5. Position the yarn on the black paper to represent the path of the earth's orbit around the sun; then glue it in place.
6. Use a yellow crayon to draw the sun's rays as shown in the illustration.
7. Use a white crayon to write the title of the model and label the poles, the seasons, the hemispheres, and the dates of the winter solstice as shown.

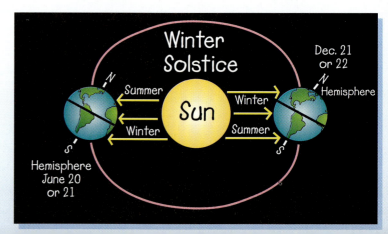

Snowmen Around The World

Imagine your classroom decorated with snowmen attired in the native dress of the world's many countries! Have each of your students select a favorite country and research the type of clothing worn by its native peoples. Then give each student an 18" x 24" sheet of white construction paper, scissors, glue, and a supply of colorful construction paper or fabric scraps. Have students cut snowmen shapes from the white construction paper and clothe their snowmen in the native costumes of the countries they researched. Post the snowmen on a bulletin board around a colored cut-out of a globe. Title the board "Snowmen Around The World" spelled with snowcapped letters. Add a border of student-made snowflakes cut from small, lace-paper doilies decorated with silver glitter so they'll glisten.

Winter Across America

Travel with your class across the United States to experience the regional differences in climate, temperature, and precipitation during the winter. Share with students Seymour Simon's book *Winter Across America* (Hyperion Books For Children). Following a discussion of the book, show a transparency (prepared ahead of time) of an enlarged national weather map from your local newspaper's weather page. Point out and discuss with students the meanings of the map's symbols. Have students use the symbols to note the different types of winter weather experienced across the country on that particular winter's day. Then distribute copies of the reproducible on page 68 so that students can make some wintry-weather computations.

Feed The Birds!

Providing food for birds is a winter custom for many people. Students can help birds survive the cold months when it's difficult for them to find food by making bird feeders filled with some of the foods listed at the right. Simple feeders can be made by hanging onion sacks or pinecones stuffed with food from tree limbs with string. A feeder can also be made from a log that's 24 inches long and four inches in diameter. Just drill large holes in the log about two inches apart and have students fill them with food. After attaching a hook to one end, students can tie the log feeder to a tree with string. Find trees on the school grounds (preferably near your classroom window) from which students can hang the feeders. Then let your youngsters create a bird-watcher's booklet in which to record their observations about the birds that gather 'round!

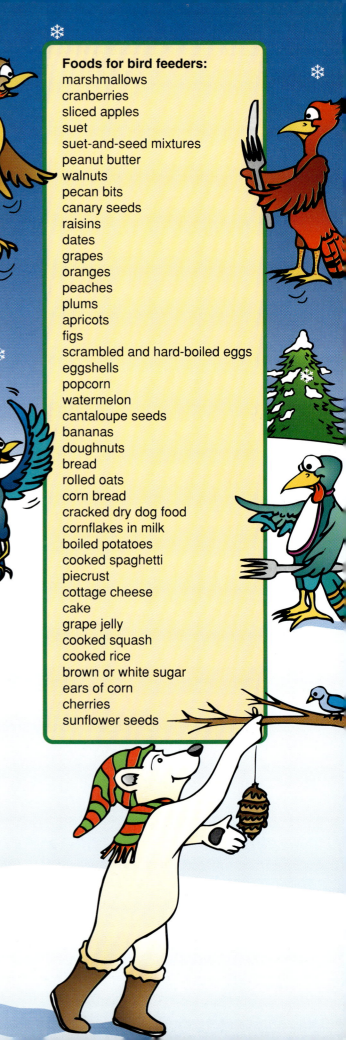

Foods for bird feeders:
marshmallows
cranberries
sliced apples
suet
suet-and-seed mixtures
peanut butter
walnuts
pecan bits
canary seeds
raisins
dates
grapes
oranges
peaches
plums
apricots
figs
scrambled and hard-boiled eggs
eggshells
popcorn
watermelon
cantaloupe seeds
bananas
doughnuts
bread
rolled oats
corn bread
cracked dry dog food
cornflakes in milk
boiled potatoes
cooked spaghetti
piecrust
cottage cheese
cake
grape jelly
cooked squash
cooked rice
brown or white sugar
ears of corn
cherries
sunflower seeds

Winter Myths

After establishing the scientific reason for winter in "The Coldest Solstice" activity on page 60, let students creatively explain why we have winter by writing myths. Explain to students that people have always wondered why natural events occur and because of this, they've created stories to satisfy their curiosity. Tell students that the Greek word *mythos* means "a spoken or written story" and that the word *myth* comes from it. Read to your class the Greek myth of Persephone from Alice Low's collection of myths in *The Macmillan Book Of Greek Gods & Heroes* (Macmillan Books For Young Readers). This myth explains why the earth has a barren, cold season. Then ask students to write and illustrate their own mythical versions about why we have winter. Videotape students acting out the stories for younger classes as they are read by a student narrator. Route the tape to students' homes so that parents can see their youngsters in action.

Winter's Hindrances

How do the colder temperatures of winter affect how well or how quickly we perform simple tasks? Let your students have fun finding the answers with this simple activity. Pair students so that at least one in the pair is wearing lace-up shoes. Give each pair five toothpicks, five grains of rice, a pencil, and paper. Direct each pair of students to perform the tasks listed below and record the times. Then give each pair a bowl of ice water that's large enough for a hand to be submerged in it. Have each member of the pair, in turn, hold his hands in the ice water for about 15–20 seconds (less if it becomes painful). Immediately after removing his hands from the ice water, have that student repeat the tasks. As students complete the experiment, allow them to warm their hands with warm—not hot—water. Discuss with students whether they thought their abilities to carry out the simple actions were hampered by their cold hands, and if so, how. Were some of the tasks easier or more difficult to do than others? Have students suggest what they could have done to make the tasks easier to perform.

Use a second hand on a clock to see how long it takes to do the following tasks:
- Tie an unlaced shoe.
- Pick up five toothpicks.
- Pick up five grains of rice.
- Write your first and last name neatly and legibly.

Magical, Snowy Adventures

Imagine a child's excitement when a winter art project he creates actually feels cold to the touch—just like snow! Read aloud *The Snow Riders* by Constance W. McGeorge (Chronicle Books), a book about a snowy creation that comes to life. Then give each student two yards of Rigid Wrap® (rolls of gauze that are powdered with plaster of paris; available at craft stores), a small cup of water, and newspaper to cover his work area. Have the student wet, shape, and smooth an animal from his gauze material. While allowing the animal creation to dry (about 30 minutes), mix and distribute painting supplies so that the student can add any desired details. Challenge each student to write an adventure story about his cold-as-snow animal which suddenly springs to life. Allow students to share their stories as the class drinks hot chocolate and eats "snowballs" made from scoops of vanilla ice cream rolled in flaked coconut.

Winter-Fun Glyphs

Youngsters love to play in the snow, go ice-skating, and participate in lots of other winter activities. Allow your students to make their favorite winter activities known to all by making *glyphs*. A glyph is a pictorial way to display detailed information through the features of a selected symbol. Provide each student with an enlarged copy of the snowman pattern on page 66, scissors, glue, crayons or markers, and colorful scraps of construction paper or fabric. Have the student use the key below to construct his winter-fun glyph on a snowman pattern. Then see "Winter Glyph Graphs" on page 65 for a graphing follow-up.

Snowman Glyph Key

1. Color of hat = favorite way to go down a snowy hill
   - green = on a sled
   - black = on skis
   - brown = on cardboard
   - red = on a snowboard
   - blue = on a snowmobile
2. Kind of hat = average length of time spent outside each day during the winter
   - baseball cap = less than 30 minutes
   - ski or stocking cap = 30 minutes to 1 hour
   - Frosty-The-Snowman top hat = 1–2 hours
   - cowboy hat = 2–3 hours
   - sombrero = more than 3 hours
3. Letter on hat = preferred way to spend time in the snow
   - W = walking in the snow
   - S = sledding
   - B = building a snowman
   - R = riding something other than a sled
   - C = constructing something other than a snowman
4. Color of scarf = what you do to warm up
   - yellow = drink hot chocolate
   - pink = sit by the fireplace
   - blue = sit by a woodstove
   - purple = cover up with a blanket
   - green = change into warm, dry clothes
5. Decorations on scarf (any color) = other winter activities in which you've participated
   - polka dots = ice-skating
   - wavy lines = riding in a horse-drawn sleigh
   - small squares = dogsledding
   - small triangles = snowball fights
   - diagonal lines = eaten "snow" ice cream
6. Number of black dots to form snowman's mouth = number of snowfalls you predict for this year
   - three dots = 3 or less
   - four dots = 4–5
   - five dots = 6–7
   - six dots = 8–9
   - seven dots = 10 or more
7. Number of buttons on your snowman's tummy = number of inches in an ideal snowfall
   - two dots = less than 1 inch
   - three dots = 1–2 inches
   - four dots = 3–4 inches
   - five dots = 5–6 inches
   - six dots = more than 6 inches
8. Now add your snowman's eyes and nose!

Weathering The Winter

Snoozing-away bears? Toughing-it-out deer? I'm-outa-here birds? How *do* animals spend the winter months? Prepare a classificatory poster about how animals weather the winter as shown. Then have your students research how animals that live in the world's cold regions survive the winter. Ask each student to choose an animal from the list provided. Challenge him to find out how it spends the winter. Does it adapt and remain in the same general area? Does it hibernate? Or does it migrate? Have the student write a brief summary of the animal's winter habits on a poster-board shape of the animal that he draws and cuts out. In addition, ask the student to write his animal's name under the correct heading on the poster. Then surround the poster with the students' animal shapes.

marmot	bighorn sheep
woodchuck	pronghorn
garden snail	mountain lion
American badger	weasel
brown bat	red fox
leopard frog	coyote
red squirrel	cardinal
brown bear	blue jay
polar bear	beaver
deer	pika
prairie dog	ant
ground squirrel	arctic tern
snowshoe hare	snow goose
ptarmigan	duck
chipmunk	bobolink
garter snake	penguin
box turtle	humpback whale
raccoon	northern fur seal
snowy owl	North American caribou
skunk	monarch butterfly

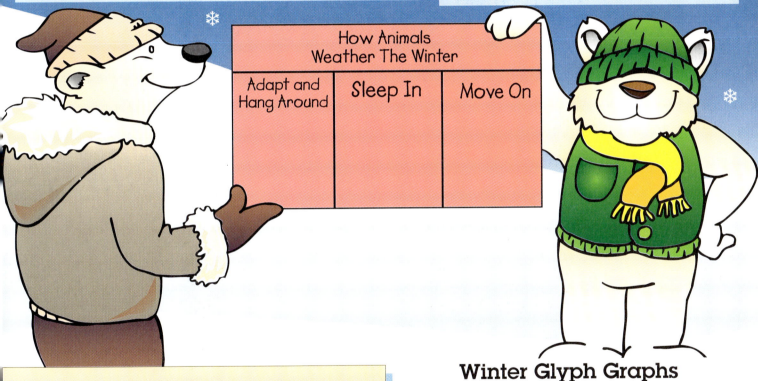

Winter Glyph Graphs

Extend the "Winter-Fun Glyphs" activity on page 64 by having small groups of students make graphs based on the glyphs. Divide your students into groups of four. Assign each group a different attribute from the glyphs to show in a picture or bar graph. For example, have one group graph students' favorite ways to go down a snowy hill. Have another group graph the number of predicted snowfalls, etc. Give each group a ruler, colored markers, and a 12" x 18" sheet of tagboard on which to draw its graph. Display the completed graphs near the snowmen glyphs on a wall or bulletin board.

The Great Icicle Race

Improve your students' study habits, social skills, or behavior with this winter-themed incentive board. Make a class supply of the icicle pattern on page 67. Write each student's (or group's) name on an icicle and tape it to the edge of your bulletin board's chalk tray. Each day that a student displays responsible behavior, turns in homework, or displays any other skill you wish to develop, have him tape another icicle onto the previous one. When a student's icicle reaches the floor, reward him with a flavored icicle on a stick—a Popsicle®!

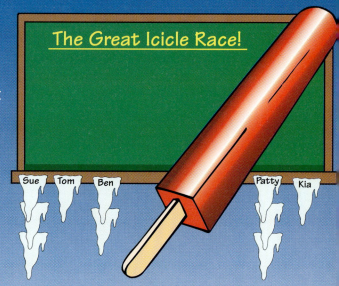

Pattern
Use with "Winter-Fun Glyphs" on page 64.

Pattern
Use with "The Coldest Solstice" on page 60.

Pattern
Use with "The Great Icicle Race" on page 66.

Name _____   Reading a chart

Oh, The Weather Outside Is Frightful

When the wind blows, we feel cooler because our bodies are losing heat. The faster the wind blows, the faster our bodies lose heat. Therefore, as wind speeds increase, we feel much colder. The relationship between wind speed and air temperature is called *wind chill,* and it determines how cold we feel.

The chart below shows how cold the air feels when wind blows at a certain speed. The darker shaded areas mean that the danger of *frostbite* (the partial freezing of some part of the body) is increasing. The lightly shaded area represents the least chance of getting frostbite, while the darkest area represents the greatest chance.

Look at the chart. If the air temperature is 20°F and the wind is blowing at a speed of 15 mph, the wind chill equals –5°F. This means that you would feel like the temperature is –5° F, and the danger of getting frostbite would be small.

Use the chart to help you work these problems. Use the back of the sheet to show your work.

1. An average low temperature for January in Helena, Montana, is 10°F. What would the wind chill be if the wind were blowing at a speed of 20 mph? _____

2. The average high temperature for January in Bismarck, North Dakota, is 20°F. If the wind chill is –18°F, what is the wind speed? _____

3. If the average temperature for the month of December in Hartford, Connecticut, is 30°F, and the wind chill is 16°F, how fast is the wind blowing? _____

4. In Fairbanks, Alaska, the average temperature for January is –10°F. If the wind is not blowing, how cold does it feel? _____

5. Thirty degrees Fahrenheit is the average temperature for February in Columbus, Ohio. If the wind were blowing at a speed of 25 mph, how cold would it feel? _____

6. If the temperature were 15°F and the wind was blowing at a speed of 27 mph, what would the wind chill be? _____

Air temp. °F	\multicolumn{9}{c}{Wind speed in miles per hour}
	0	5	10	15	20	25	30	35	40
	\multicolumn{9}{c}{Equivalent wind chill temperatures}
35	35	32	22	16	12	8	6	4	3
30	30	27	16	9	4	1	–2	–4	–5
25	25	22	10	2	–3	–7	–10	–12	–13
20	20	16	3	–5	–10	–15	–18	–20	–21
15	15	11	–3	–11	–17	–22	–25	–27	–29
10	10	6	–9	–18	–24	–29	–33	–35	–37
5	5	0	–15	–25	–31	–36	–41	–43	–45
0	0	–5	–22	–31	–39	–44	–49	–52	–53
–5	–5	–10	–27	–38	–46	–51	–56	–58	–60
–10	–10	–15	–34	–45	–53	–59	–64	–67	–69
–15	–15	–21	–40	–51	–60	–66	–71	–74	–76
–20	–20	–26	–46	–58	–67	–74	–79	–82	–84
–25	–25	–31	–52	–65	–74	–81	–86	–89	–92

7. What is the air temperature if the wind speed is 5 mph and the wind chill is 16°F? _____

8. If the wind chill is –18°F, the wind speed could be 30 mph in one place and 15 mph in another. What would the temperatures need to be for these two places? _____

9. What are the two possible temperatures and wind speed conditions if the wind chill is –20°F? _____

10. For the air temperature and the wind chill to be the same, what does the wind speed have to be? _____

Bonus Box: Find three different wind chill temperatures that appear four times in the chart. Give the air temperature and wind speed conditions under which they occur.

©1996 The Education Center, Inc. • *DECEMBER* • TEC201 • Key p. 96

Note To The Teacher: Use this reproducible with the "Winter Across America" activity on page 61.

Name _____ Research contract

Weathering The Winter

Discover all kinds of exciting, new facts about the winter season as you make the temperature rise on the thermometer below. As you complete each activity on the snowflakes, color in another section of mercury on the thermometer with a red crayon or marker. By the time you color the last section, the temperature should be warming its way toward spring!

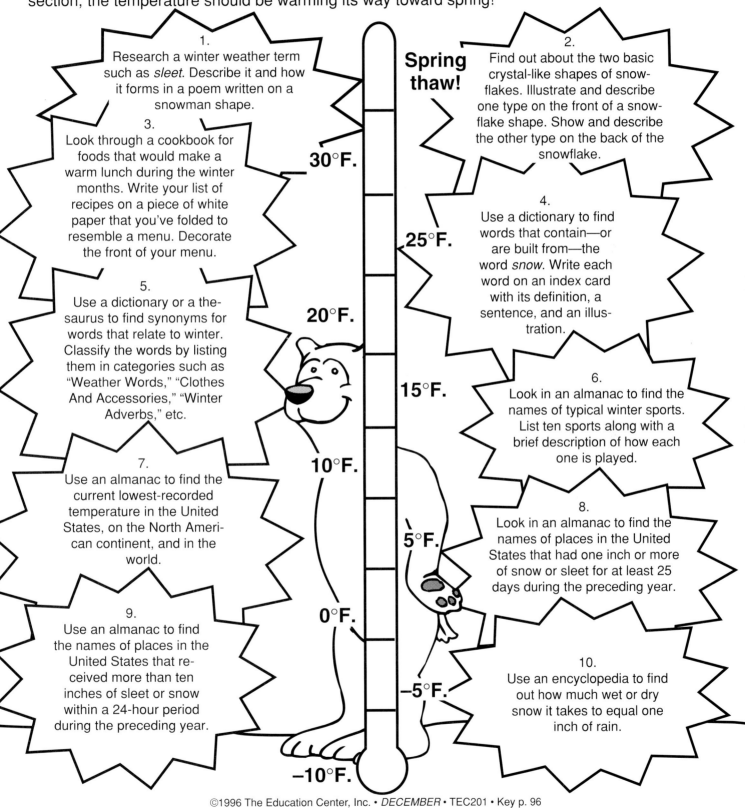

1. Research a winter weather term such as *sleet*. Describe it and how it forms in a poem written on a snowman shape.

2. Find out about the two basic crystal-like shapes of snowflakes. Illustrate and describe one type on the front of a snowflake shape. Show and describe the other type on the back of the snowflake.

3. Look through a cookbook for foods that would make a warm lunch during the winter months. Write your list of recipes on a piece of white paper that you've folded to resemble a menu. Decorate the front of your menu.

4. Use a dictionary to find words that contain—or are built from—the word *snow*. Write each word on an index card with its definition, a sentence, and an illustration.

5. Use a dictionary or a thesaurus to find synonyms for words that relate to winter. Classify the words by listing them in categories such as "Weather Words," "Clothes And Accessories," "Winter Adverbs," etc.

6. Look in an almanac to find the names of typical winter sports. List ten sports along with a brief description of how each one is played.

7. Use an almanac to find the current lowest-recorded temperature in the United States, on the North American continent, and in the world.

8. Look in an almanac to find the names of places in the United States that had one inch or more of snow or sleet for at least 25 days during the preceding year.

9. Use an almanac to find the names of places in the United States that received more than ten inches of sleet or snow within a 24-hour period during the preceding year.

10. Use an encyclopedia to find out how much wet or dry snow it takes to equal one inch of rain.

©1996 The Education Center, Inc. • DECEMBER • TEC201 • Key p. 96

Note To The Teacher: Provide students with the following: dictionaries, thesauruses, encyclopedias, a variety of cookbooks, and several copies of a current world almanac.

69

Gumption, Grit, And A Goal
Thematic Activities On Inventors And Inventing

Where would the world be without inventors? With large doses of gumption and grit—plus a single-minded pursuit of a goal—an inventor uses his or her observation skills and the ability to generate new ideas to change the world. Celebrate the special December dates in the history of inventing (see the box below) by embarking on an ingenious study of inventions and the people who create them.

by Elizabeth Lindsay, Casimir Badynee, and Tammie Boone

Necessity Is The Mother Of Invention

As you begin a study of inventors and inventing, your students may ask, "What makes an invention an invention? Who can be an inventor?" Use the following activity to answer these questions and help students see that inventions are all around us. Give each child a brown paper lunch bag. For a homework assignment, direct the student to take the bag home and fill it with 10 to 15 small items that he considers "inventive inventions" (for example, a Band-Aid®, a safety pin, a paper clip, etc.). As a student collects each item, he should list its name on the bag and write one sentence that explains the need it answers and why he thinks it's inventive.

The next day have students share some of the items in their bags with the class. Lead them to understand that even the simplest of things is an invention that started out as an idea in someone's head. Some inventions are ideas that have never been thought of before, while others are ideas that have been improved or changed in some way. All of the ideas meet a need. Becoming an inventor is just an idea—and a need—away!

1. comb
2. marker
3. cotton ball
4. screwdriver
5. paper clip
6. clothespin
7. spatula
8. envelope
9. safety pin
10. laundry-detergent scoop

Special December Dates In The History Of Inventing

Dec. 8, 1765—Birthdate of Eli Whitney, inventor of the cotton gin

Dec. 9, 1886—Birthdate of Clarence Birdseye, inventor of frozen foods

Dec. 10, 1851—Birthdate of Melvil Dewey, creator of the Dewey decimal book-classification system

Dec. 10, 1896—The day on which Alfred Nobel, inventor of dynamite, died.

Dec. 12, 1901—The day on which Guglielmo Marconi sent the first transatlantic radio signal

Dec. 17, 1903—The day of the Wright brothers' first successful, heavier-than-air powered flight

Dec. 27, 1822—Birthdate of Louis Pasteur, creator of a rabies vaccine and person for whom the pasteurization process is named

Dec. 28, 1869—The day on which William F. Semple received a patent for his invention, chewing gum

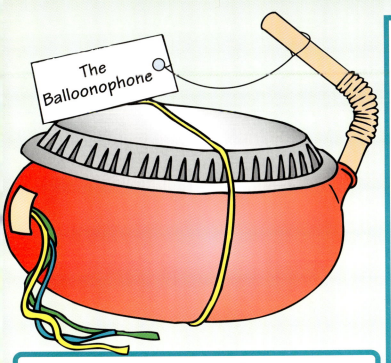

A Weed Is A Flower...

One of the most prolific inventors in American history was scientist, artist, horticulturist, and teacher George Washington Carver. Dr. Carver discovered more than 300 uses for one plant, the peanut. Read aloud *A Weed Is A Flower: The Life Of George Washington Carver* by Aliki (Simon & Schuster Books For Young Readers) or *A Pocketful Of Goobers: A Story About George Washington Carver* by Barbara Mitchell (Carolrhoda Books, Inc.). Dr. Carver reportedly once said that a weed is a flower growing in the wrong place. Have students discuss what they believe this remark might tell about Carver's attitude toward inventing. Is there a link between this attitude and the huge number of uses Carver found for the peanut plant? Have each student write his response to this question in his journal. (For fun, let students munch on salted peanuts while they write.) Then have students discuss what the remark might convey about Carver's attitude about people.

Creative Contrivances

Create something from nothing? Well, not exactly. Many inventive ideas come from opening up your mind to new ways of using old things. To help students understand that inventing is really a process of creative problem solving, divide them into groups. Give each group a piece of paper and instructions to use only the paper to invent a container that will hold water. Let groups share their water-holding inventions. Point out that even the simplest of ideas can become the cleverest of inventions.

Next direct students to collect various items from home, such as yarn, scraps of fabric and wallpaper, toothpicks, straws, pipe cleaners, buttons, etc. (Or use the items collected in "Necessity Is The Mother Of Invention" on page 70.) Divide students into new groups; then provide each group with masking tape, glue, scissors, rulers, and pencils. Challenge the groups to combine their collected items and use them to create a new invention that meets one of the challenges listed below. Let groups introduce their creative contrivances to the class. Follow up this activity with the bulletin-board idea on page 72.

Challenges:
- Invent a new organizer for your school supplies so they don't get lost or damaged in your desk.
- Invent a safe toy for a two-year-old child.
- Invent a noisemaker that will keep your dog from chewing on your favorite pair of shoes.

Picture-Perfect Inventions

Shine a spotlight on your students' creative talents with this bulletin-board idea. Bring a camera to school and take a close-up photograph of each invention created by groups in the "Creative Contrivances" idea on page 71. Then take a photo of each group of inventors. After you've developed the photos, duplicate the reproducible frames on page 78 (two frames per group). Have members from each group color their group's two frames with colorful markers; then glue the groups' photos—trimming them if necessary—inside the frames. Enlarge, color, and cut out the character on page 77. Mount him on a board with the framed photos and the title.

Weird And Wacky

To the inventor, his creation may seem like just the answer for a particular need. However, to the public, the invention may seem just plain silly. One book that explores strange contraptions that never made it into invention history is *Guess Again: More Weird And Wacky Inventions* by Jim Murphy (Bradbury Press). This fascinating book—formatted as a guessing game—illustrates some of the unusual inventions people have dreamed up over the last two centuries (for example, a life preserver for horses, a mechanical golf instructor, a machine for patting a baby to sleep). Divide your class into groups. Show the groups one of the illustrations from Murphy's book; then have them discuss the picture and guess the purpose of the invention. After each group has shared its ideas, reveal the machine's true purpose by reading aloud Murphy's explanation.

Room For Improvement

The saying that "there's always room for improvement" is especially true in the field of inventing. Modern inventions rarely result from the efforts of one inventor. Inventions such as the telephone have been modified and improved by many creative minds over the years. Demonstrate this to students by enlarging pictures of telephones from different historical periods from an encyclopedia. Post the pictures; then discuss with students the improvements that have been made over time. Brainstorm a list of other modern inventions that have been improved over time, such as the television, the computer, and the airplane. What makes them "better" than ones used years ago? Lead students to see that *better* can mean many things: easier to use, smaller, designed with a greater number of features or functions, more attractive, faster, etc.

Next divide students into groups. Give each group a copy of page 79 and a common object such as a wallet, notebook, pair of sunglasses, etc. Have groups use the steps on the reproducible to come up with a way to improve its object. Hold a session during which groups share their plans with the class. As a follow-up homework assignment, have each student develop a plan for improving a common object found in his home.

What Do We *Really* Need?

Put on your thinking caps for this mind-stretching activity! Divide students into several small groups. Have each group make a list of inventions or machines that people really need. Next have the group list inventions that people could do without. Meet as a class and have groups share their lists. If time permits, have each group list the five most important inventions yet to be invented.

Inventions People Really Need	Inventions People Could Do Without
telephone X-ray machine wheel television computer	TV remote dishwasher popcorn popper microwave oven

73

Doors To Discovery

Who better to inspire your students to discover their inventive talents than creative minds from the past? To get students interested in researching famous inventors, share a few fascinating stories found in any of these books:

Small Inventions That Make A Big Difference (National Geographic Society)
Steven Caney's Invention Book by Steven Caney (Workman Publishing)
Outward Dreams: Black Inventors And Their Inventions by Jim Haskins (Walker and Company)
Women Inventors And Their Discoveries by Ethlie Ann Vare and Greg Ptacek (The Oliver Press, Inc.)
Mistakes That Worked by Charlotte Jones (Doubleday & Company, Inc.)
Dreamers And Doers: Inventors Who Changed The World by Norman Richards (Atheneum)

Next write these categories on the board, leaving space underneath each one: Health and Medicine, Science and Technology, Communication, Leisure Living, and Transportation. Have students brainstorm inventions for you to list under each category. Then give each student a copy of the list of inventors on page 77. Have each child choose an inventor to research. Give each child six large index cards to label *Who? What? When? Where? How?* and *Why?* After students have finished their research, have them complete the following steps to create some truly inventive projects.

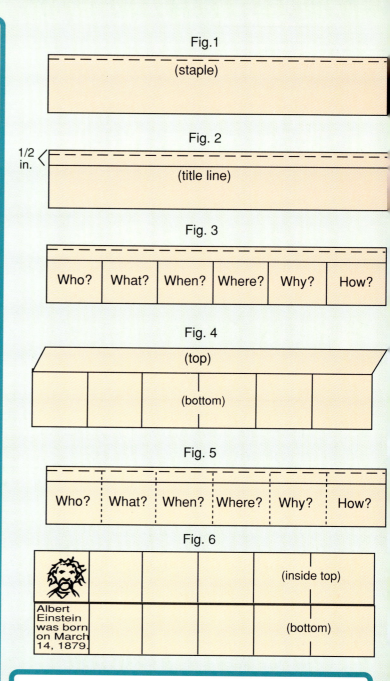

Making A "Door To Discovery"
1. Staple together two sentence strips at the top as shown in figure 1.
2. Use a ruler to draw a line 1/2-inch from the stapled edge of the top strip (see figure 2).
3. Use the ruler to divide the top strip into six equal sections as shown in figure 3.
4. Label each section, or door, as shown in figure 3.
5. Repeat step 3 on the bottom sentence strip as shown in figure 4.
6. Cut the dividing lines between the doors on the top strip as shown in figure 5. Stop the cutting lines at the staples.
7. Open each door. On the bottom flap, write the facts that will answer that door's question. On the top flap, draw and color a picture to illustrate your facts. Complete this step for the remaining five doors.
8. After sharing your project with the class, pin it on a bulletin board.

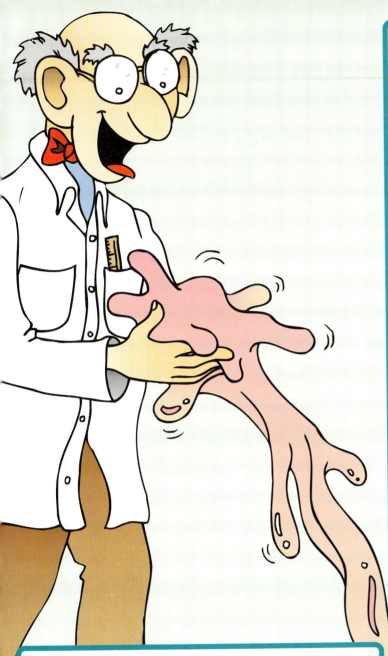

Eureka!
(What Did I Just Invent?)

Inventions are often discovered by mere chance. For example, in 1970 Dr. Spencer Sylver discovered an adhesive that "sticks without sticking." But his company could find no use for the stuff. Ten years later, one of his co-workers—who was also a church choir member—needed a way to mark the pages of his music book without damaging them. He put a thin layer of the adhesive onto small page markers, and the Post-It™ note was born! Discuss this story with your students. Then divide them into groups to complete a hands-on, creative-thinking project:

Materials for each group: 25 ml water, 50 ml cornstarch, cup, spoon or fork, waxed paper, additional water (optional)

Steps:
1. Pour the 25 ml water into the cup.
2. Add the cornstarch a little at a time, stirring constantly.
3. When the mixture becomes too thick to stir, remove it from the cup and knead it on the waxed paper.
4. Add a few drops of water if the mixture is too crumbly.

After groups explore and experiment with the glop, challenge them to pretend they are a team of inventors that has just invented this stuff. Have groups propose ways the glop could help the public; then have them write proposals for their inventions. Set aside a time for groups to share their "glop gimmicks."

Inventive Literature

Spread the spirit of inventing with these wonderful books on inventions and inventors.

Fiction
The Gadget War by Betsy Duffey (Viking Children's Books)
Burton And The Giggle Machine by Dorothy Haas (Simon & Schuster Children's Books)
Egg-Drop Blues by Jacqueline T. Banks (Houghton Mifflin Company)

Nonfiction
The Picture History Of Great Inventors by Gillian Clements (Alfred A. Knopf Books For Young Readers)
Experimenting With Inventions by Robert Gardner (Franklin Watts, Inc.)
The Problem Solvers: People Who Turned Problems Into Products by Nathan Aaseng (The Lerner Group)
The Rejects: People And Products That Outsmarted The Experts by Nathan Aaseng (The Lerner Group)

An Invention Convention

After students have read about inventors—both famous and not-so-famous—they're sure to catch the inventing bug. Plan a classroom-wide Invention Convention that will highlight the creative genius in each of your students. Just follow this step-by-step plan:

Step 1: Make a master copy of the Invention Convention project outline on page 80; then fill in the due dates and duplicate a copy for each student. Duplicate a copy of the Inventor's Plan on page 81 and five to ten copies of the Inventor's Daily Log on page 80 for each child.

Step 2: Go over the Invention Convention outline with students. Provide time for students to make their Bug Books. Set a due date a week from this session during which students can share their books.

Step 3: Hold a session during which students discuss and rank the items they've listed in their Bug Books. Allow time for interested students to pair up with classmates to brainstorm ideas for their inventions. Then distribute student copies of the Inventor's Plan (page 81) and the Inventor's Daily Log (page 80). Let students make their Inventor's Daily Log booklets by stapling their pages inside construction-paper covers.

Step 4: Allow a week (or more) for students to complete their invention plans and make their models. Remind them to take notes in their logs each day.

Step 5: On the day of the Invention Convention, let each student share the model of his invention with the class. Post each student's labeled sketch on a bulletin board titled "Our Intent Was To Invent!" Be sure to invite parents, other classes, and school personnel to your Invention Convention.

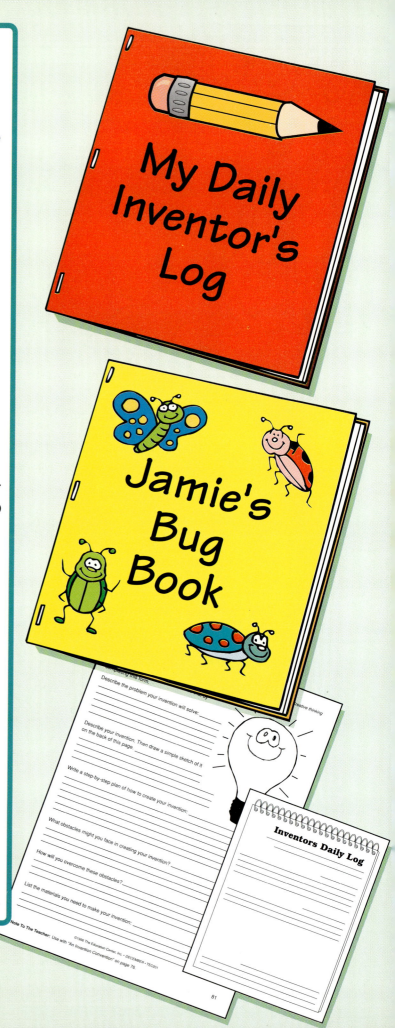

Pattern
Use with "Picture-Perfect Inventions" on page 72.

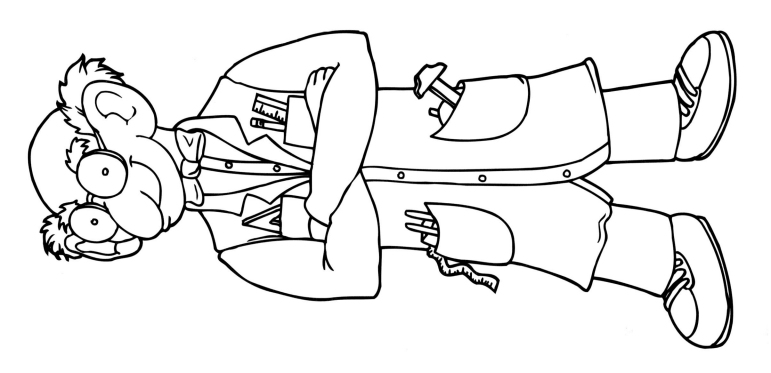

©1996 The Education Center, Inc. • DECEMBER • TEC201

Their Intent Was To Invent!

Below are the names of some famous inventors. Choose one inventor to research. Look for answers to these questions as you research: *Who? What? Why? When? Where? How?*

Charles Babbage	Benjamin Franklin	Elijah McCoy
Benjamin Banneker	Robert Fulton	Samuel Morse
Alexander Graham Bell	Robert Goddard	Elizabeth Lucas Pinckney
Louis Braille	Johannes Gutenberg	Norbert Rillieux
Chester F. Carlson	Ruth Handler	Wilhelm Röntgen
Wallace Hume Carothers	Heinrich Rudolf Hertz	Christopher L. Sholes
Martha Coston	Elias Howe	Igor Sikorsky
Louis-Jacques Mandé Daguerre	Joseph-Marie Jacquard	George Stephenson
Gottlieb Daimler	Percy Julian	Evangelista Torricelli
Rudolf Diesel	Lewis Latimer	Count Alessandro Volta
John Boyd Dunlop	Etienne Lenoir	Madam C. J. Walker
George Eastman	Hans Lippershey	Eli Whitney
Thomas Alva Edison	Jan Matzeliger	Granville T. Woods
Fannie Merritt Farmer	Cyrus Hall McCormick	Vladimir Zworykin

©1996 The Education Center, Inc. • DECEMBER • TEC201

Note To The Teacher: Use the list of inventors with "Doors To Discovery" on page 74.

77

Patterns
Use with "Picture-Perfect Inventions" on page 72.

©1996 The Education Center, Inc. • *DECEMBER* • TEC201

©1996 The Education Center, Inc. • *DECEMBER* • TEC201

Group Members: _____   *Critical thinking*

Make It Better!

How about a computer that also makes milkshakes?

Pretend that you work for an inventor who is always looking for ways to improve everyday objects around us. This inventor has asked your group to come up with a way to improve an everyday invention. After your teacher gives you the invention (or a picture of it), work as a group to complete the form. Be prepared to share your solution with the class.

Your group's object: _____

What are some possible ways to improve the object? List as many possibilities as you can: _____
_____
_____
_____
_____
_____

What problems do you face in improving the object in the ways you listed? _____
_____
_____
_____

What is the best improvement you came up with? _____

Explain why it is the best choice. _____
_____
_____

How will this improved invention help people? _____
_____
_____

There are many ways to name an invention:
- Name it for the way it works: typewriter, skateboard, hair dryer
- Give it a clever name to attract customers: Silly Putty®, Jell-O®, Hula-Hoop®
- Name it after the inventor: Ford automobile, Morse code, Ferris wheel
- Name it after its contents: rubber cement, peanut butter, ice cream
- Name it to sound technical: Formula 400, Model X15

What will you name your new-and-improved invention? _____

Draw a sketch of your improved invention on the back of this page. Label its parts.

©1996 The Education Center, Inc. • *DECEMBER* • TEC201

Note To The Teacher: Use with "Room For Improvement" on page 73. Each student group will need a copy of this page and a different commonplace object (or a picture of one) such as a wallet, notebook, bookbag, etc.

Name _____

Planning and completing a project

Invention Convention Project Outline

1. To begin, cut three or four sheets of notebook paper in half. Staple the half pages together to make a small booklet. Decorate the cover of your booklet to read "Bug Book."

2. Carry your Bug Book with you everywhere for one week. Inside it, keep a running list of things that really bug you. On _____, be prepared

                                                                                                                date
   to share your list with the class.

3. During the sharing session, feel free to add some of your classmates' ideas to your Bug Book. At the end of the session, rank your ideas to find out which item bugs you the most.

4. Take some time to brainstorm ideas for an invention that will help to solve your top-ranked Bug Book problem. Ask a friend or family member to help you brainstorm ideas if you like.

5. Complete your copy of the "Inventor's Plan." Take the form home so that you can start gathering the necessary supplies. Your invention is due _____.

date

6. Notes can be the proof an inventor needs to show the world that he/she deserves the patent rights to the invention. As you work on your invention, keep daily notes in your Inventor's Daily Log.

7. Make a model of your invention. Be sure that it is large enough to be seen, but not so large that it will be difficult to bring to school. If needed, you may make a scale model. Be sure your invention is safe and that it will not be too expensive to make.

8. Before you present your invention to the class, you should name it. There are many ways to name an invention:
   - Name it for the way it works: typewriter, skateboard, hair dryer
   - Give it a clever name to attract customers: Silly Putty®, Jell-O®, Hula-Hoop®
   - Name it after the inventor: Ford automobile, Morse code, Ferris wheel
   - Name it after its contents: rubber cement, peanut butter, ice cream
   - Name it to sound technical: Formula 400, Model X15

9. Inventors usually make drawings of their inventions to show how they work. Draw a simple, labeled sketch (larger than the one you drew on the "Inventor's Plan") showing all the parts of your invention.

10. The Invention Convention will be held on _____. Be prepared

                                                                                                            date
    to present your model and sketch and explain your invention to the class.

Inventor's Daily Log

Inventor: _____

Today's date: _____

Description of today's accomplishments: _____
_____
_____

Results of any testing or experiments: _____
_____
_____

Sketch of my observations:

Goal for tomorrow: _____
_____

©1996 The Education Center, Inc. • *DECEMBER* • TEC201

Note To The Teacher: Use both of these reproducibles with "An Invention Convention" on page 76. Fill in the due dates on "Invention Convention Project Outline" before duplicating a class supply.

Name _____   *Creative thinking*

Inventor's Plan

If your intent is to invent, first you must create a plan of action for your bright idea. You can do that by completing this form.

Describe the problem your invention will solve: _____
_____
_____
_____
_____

Describe your invention. Then draw a simple sketch of it on the back of this page. _____
_____
_____
_____
_____

Write a step-by-step plan of how to create your invention: _____
_____
_____
_____
_____
_____
_____

What obstacles might you face in creating your invention? _____
_____
_____
_____

How will you overcome these obstacles? _____
_____
_____
_____

List the materials you need to make your invention: _____
_____
_____

©1996 The Education Center, Inc. • *DECEMBER* • TEC201

Note To The Teacher: Use with "An Invention Convention" on page 76.

Name _____   *Critical thinking, vocabulary*

Confusing Conundrums About Creative Contrivances

Below is a list of riddles that describe some inventions with which you should be very familiar. But the riddles contain words you probably won't know. No problem! Use Noah Webster's invention—the dictionary—to look up the words you don't know. Then try to guess the identity of each mystery invention. Write the answer in the numbered lightbulb.

1. Once I was a wad of grass, leaves, or tree sap. I was chewed for relaxation and enjoyment. Doctors once warned that I would "exhaust salivary glands and cause the intestines to stick together." What am I?

2. I am a conundrum of interlocking pieces once made of wood. Now I am found in every size, shape, and color. I was invented by John Spilsbury in 1767. What am I?

3. I am a device with a pointed apex and a circular twist at the bend. I was created after my inventor, Walter Hunt, twisted a piece of wire for three hours. What am I?

4. I am a spherical-shaped object made of sticks or tubes of wood, plastic, or metal. I have a piece of graphite in the center. I am an excellent writing implement. What am I?

5. I am an elastic fetter discovered by Thomas Hancock in 1820. He created me by slicing a series of rings from a bottle made from the sap of rubber trees. What am I?

6. At first I was composed of bristles that were wedged and glued into holes bored into pieces of bone. I was invented by William Addis in 1770 because he was tired of using a rag. What am I?

7. I am an object on which people repose for one-third of their lives. Once I was made of nothing more than a pile of leaves or straw. But now I can be made of feathers, cotton, even water! What am I?

8. I am nothing more than flakes of flattened, boiled wheat kernels devised to "break the fast." I have made my inventors, Mr. Post and Mr. Kellogg, quite affluent. What am I?

9. I am a viscous substance. Prehistoric people made me from raw eggs, dried blood, boiled bones, or sticky juices from plants and insects. You could say that people get stuck on me. What am I?

10. I was first made for miners from the canvas of tents and wagons. I was so tough even two horses couldn't pull me apart. I was invented in 1847 by Mr. Levi Strauss. What am I?

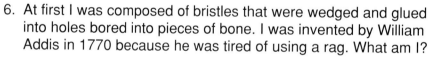
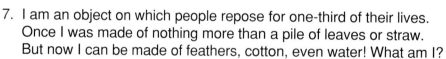
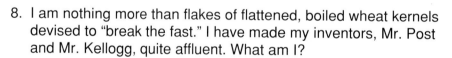
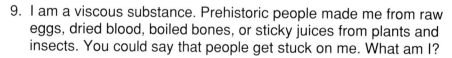

Bonus Box: On the back of this page, list ten other substances that are viscous. Or make a list of ten people you consider to be affluent. Or list ten other items that could each be used as a fetter.

Name _____ Critical thinking

Square Pegs

Ever hear the phrase, "You can't fit a square peg in a round hole"? In each group of inventions below, one of the items is a square peg—it doesn't belong in that group. Circle the word in each numbered row that doesn't fit. On the line, write a phrase explaining why the other three items go together.

1. life preserver — doughnut — Hula-Hoop® — plate
2. steel — chewing gum — glue — Velcro®
3. comb — bicycle — chair — bed
4. laser — candle — fireworks — can opener
5. Walkman™ — CD player — tuning fork — lightbulb
6. bifocals — microscope — camera — aspirin
7. hot-air balloon — parachute — Frisbee® — camera
8. basket — saw — laser — knife
9. rubber band — windshield wipers — vacuum cleaner — toothpaste
10. comb — zipper — dentures — toothpick
11. bicycle — shopping cart — canoe — roller skates
12. potato chips — french fries — barbed wire — television
13. ruler — thermometer — telephone — clock
14. abacus — typewriter — computer — calculator
15. compass — clock — map — traffic light

Bonus Box: Write another grouping like the ones above. Give it to a friend to see whether he or she can find the square peg.

©1996 The Education Center, Inc. • DECEMBER • TEC201 • Key p. 96

83

KWANZAA TIME!

Help your students join the 18 million people in the United States who celebrate Kwanzaa each year. The following activities will reinforce basic principles that encourage harmony and pride in the African American community, as well as celebrate the rich history and achievements of African Americans.

by Simone Lepine

What Is Kwanzaa?

Kwanzaa is a fairly new holiday created in 1966 by Dr. Maulana Karenga. Kwanzaa is a mixture of African, African American, Afro-Caribbean, and Afro-Latin customs. Dr. Karenga based the holiday on seven principles called *Nguzo Saba*. A new principle is celebrated each day of Kwanzaa. The seven days of Kwanzaa begin on December 26 and correspond to a harvest and celebration time in Africa. It is important to note that Kwanzaa is not an alternative to or replacement for Christmas, but rather a celebration to enrich cultural harmony and pride. Families are encouraged to personalize their celebrations of Kwanzaa with their own family traditions.

Kwanzaa Symbols

The symbols used during Kwanzaa represent ideas and thoughts that cannot be seen or touched, but bring great meaning to the celebration. Listed below are seven symbols followed by activities on this page and on pages 85–86 (excluding mazao) to introduce them to your students.

- **Zawadi** .... gifts
- **Mkeka** .... a woven mat
- **Kikombe Cha Umoja** .... unity cup
- **Mishumaa Saba** .... seven candles
- **Kinara** .... candleholder
- **Muhindi** .... ears of corn
- **Mazao** .... crops (gather some locally grown foods)

Kwanzaa Gift Giving

Like other holidays, Kwanzaa includes gift giving. *Zawadi* (gifts) are given from the head, heart, and hands. Children give handmade gifts, while parents usually give educational gifts. Have students create zawadi for their parents. Set up an art center containing red, green, and black construction paper, glue, scissors, markers, glitter, yarn, etc. Instruct the students to create Kwanzaa cards using the materials in the center. Have a sample card displayed in the center showing both sides of the card decorated, a Kwanzaa greeting on the front, and a brief message inside.

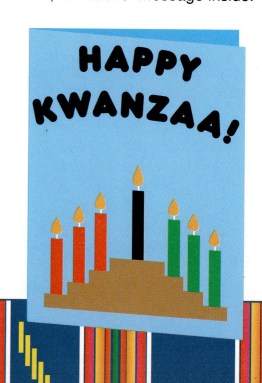

Weaving History

The first symbol of Kwanzaa is the *mkeka* (a woven mat) which symbolizes African American tradition and history. Have your students create their own mkekas while learning about their family histories. Send students home with the following list of questions: From which country did my ancestors originate? Who was the first known relative to come to the United States? How long has our family been in this country? Why did our family come to the United States? Also have the students bring family photos (if available) to school. Have the students use their answers to write brief family histories. Let the students share their work; then display the family histories and photos on a bulletin board.

To create the mkekas, have each student follow these directions:

1. Fold an 8 1/2" x 11" piece of black construction paper in half lengthwise. Starting at the fold, cut strips one inch in width, stopping your cuts one inch from the end. Unfold the paper.
2. Use a ruler to measure one-inch-wide strips on a red sheet and a green sheet of construction paper. Cut them out. Weave the strips over and under the slats of the black paper, alternating red and green.
3. Use small dabs of glue to secure the strips to the black paper. Add your mkeka to the family histories display.

Step 1   **Step 2**

Unity Cup

Each day during Kwanzaa, a *libation* (water, wine, or juice) is poured into the *kikombe cha umoja,* or unity cup. Everyone sips from the cup to symbolize the unity of the family and community. After drinking from the cup, the family discusses great African Americans. Discuss the seven principles of Kwanzaa on page 92 with the students. Have each student choose a famous African American to research; then have the student write why the person is famous and what Kwanzaa principle he or she emulates on a long strip of white paper. Next have each student create a unity cup in honor of the famous African American he researched using the directions below. Finally instruct each student to roll up his strip and place it in his unity cup. Display the cups in the library for others to read.

Materials for each student: one cardboard toilet-paper tube, two large paper cups, aluminum foil, glue, scissors, and permanent markers

1. Glue the cardboard tube to the bottom of one cup.
2. Take the other cup and cut its height down to one inch.
3. Glue the bottom of the one-inch cup to the other end of the tube with the opening facing downward.
4. Cover the entire cup with aluminum foil. Write the famous African American's name on the cup with a black permanent marker. Use other colored markers to decorate the cup.

Muhindi

Children are an important part of the Kwanzaa celebration. They are symbolized by *muhindi,* or ears of corn. Each kernel on the corn symbolizes future generations of children. The muhindi are placed on the family's mkeka. Ask your students what is meant by the phrase "children are the hope of the future." List their ideas on the board. Next give each student a copy of page 94. Have students complete the activity; then let volunteers share their dreams in class.

As a follow-up, have students create their own muhindi using the directions below. Divide the students into small groups. Provide orange, red, yellow, and blue paint for each group. Give each student one 12" x 18" sheet of white and one sheet of brown construction paper, glue, scissors, and the following instructions:

1. Fold the white paper lengthwise; then draw an ear of corn with the top of the ear at the fold. Cut out the corn. You should have two ears of corn attached by a fold at the top.
2. Dip your index finger into different colors of paint; then press your finger on the top ear of corn to create kernels. Cover the entire ear.
3. Cut out two husks from the brown paper. Glue them to the back of the bottom ear.
4. Open up the corn and write one wish for the future of the world inside.

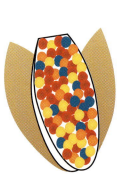

Shedding Light On Kwanzaa

The *kinara* (a wooden candleholder) and *mishumaa saba* (candles) are important symbols of Kwanzaa. The kinara holds seven candles—one for each of the seven principles of Nguzo Saba. The center and first candle to be lit on the kinara is black, representing the descendants of the African people. Three red candles to the left of the black candle symbolize the struggles ancestors of the African people faced in their fight for freedom. Three green candles to the right of the black candle symbolize the green lands of Africa and hope for the future. A new candle is lit each day (alternating red and green).

Divide the class into groups of three or four students to make classroom kinaras. Give each group a shoebox; tape; brown construction paper; scissors; black, green, and red markers; glue; one copy of page 92; and seven copies of page 93. First instruct the groups to cover their boxes with the brown paper; then have them use page 92 and the directions on page 93 to complete their kinaras. Display the kinaras throughout the room during your study of Kwanzaa.

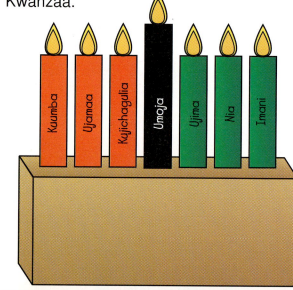

Nguzo Saba: The Seven Principles Of Kwanzaa

Kwanzaa is based upon seven principles called Nguzo Saba. *Nguzo* is Swahili for principles and *Saba* means seven. The seven principles emphasize unity and cooperation within the family, the community, the race, and the nation. A different principle is shared each day of Kwanzaa beginning December 26 and ending January 1. The Kwanzaa symbols listed on page 84 are used during the celebration of Nguzo Saba. Although Nguzo Saba is designed to help African Americans develop an understanding of their past and create a path to the future, all races can benefit from their ideals. Give each student a copy of page 92 and discuss each principle. Then use the activities on this page and pages 88–91 to celebrate Nguzo Saba.

Day 1: Umoja (Unity) No, You Can't / Yes, I Can!

This activity helps demonstrate the power of unified voices. Pick one student to start chanting, "Yes, I can." Have the rest of the class chant in unison, "No, you can't." While everyone is chanting, signal one child to switch from saying, "No, you can't," to saying, "Yes, I can." Keep signaling students to switch until there is only one child left chanting, "No, you can't." Ask the students who chanted alone at the beginning and end of the activity how they felt. Then have students share how it felt as more classmates joined them in the "Yes, I can" chant. Tell students about the Montgomery Bus Boycott of 1955–56 led by Dr. Martin Luther King, Jr., and how being unified made it successful. For over a year, the black citizens of Montgomery, Alabama, did not ride the public buses in protest of the system of segregation used on the buses. About 75 percent of the bus riders in Montgomery were black. Ask students what would happen to a business if 75 percent of its customers left. Discuss other forms of unified protests during the civil rights movement of the 1950s and '60s, such as sit-ins, freedom rides, and marches.

Day 2: Kujichagulia (Self-Determination)
I Am Free

On this day, the family reflects on their cultural heritage and their hopes and dreams for the future. Have the students get out their "Dreams For The Future" reproducibles (page 94) from the "Muhindi" activity page 86. Select students to list their dreams on the board. Next have students share what they know about slave life. Discuss how a slave's future was determined by the plantation owner. If possible, share excerpts from *To Be A Slave* by Julius Lester (Scholastic Inc.) for a realistic depiction of slave life. Have students suggest what a child slave might dream; then write their suggestions on the board beside the dreams listed previously. Let students compare the lists for any similarities.

Close this activity by having each student write a free-verse poem called "I Can Dream." Instruct students to use the dreams they listed on page 94 for ideas. Tell students that each poem should have at least five lines, with the last line stating, "I am free so my dreams are endless." Encourage students to illustrate their poems; then mount the poetry on a bulletin board.

Day 3: Ujima (Collective Work And Responsibility)
Design A Boat That Floats And A Tower That Towers

On this day the family reflects on how much can be accomplished when people work together. Divide the students into groups of two. Give each group a sheet of aluminum foil. Have each group use the foil to design a boat that will hold the most pennies. Place each group's boat in a large container of water. Add one penny at a time to each boat until there is only one boat left floating. Discuss what it was like to work with a partner. Did it make the job easier? Did your partner have ideas that you hadn't thought of using?

Keeping the same groups of two, challenge students to build the highest tower out of one piece of paper. Allow only scissors to be used in making the towers. Tell students that the towers must be able to stand freely for at least ten seconds. As a class, have groups share what it was like working together a second time. Was it easier? Was your group successful? Why?

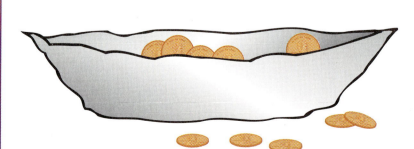
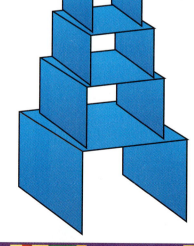

Day 4: Ujamaa (Cooperative Economics) Economic Web

The fourth day focuses on the importance of supporting local stores and starting businesses in the community. For this activity you will need a ball of yarn and a nametag for each student. Write a different name of a local business on each nametag. Have the students form a circle; then give each student a nametag. Explain that they represent business owners who are all from the same community.

Start the game by giving the ball of yarn to one student. Instruct him to grab the end of the yarn and continue holding it until the end of the game. Then have him toss the rest of the yarn to a person he wants to conduct business with. When that person gets the ball of yarn, she pulls the yarn taunt, holds on to her section, and then tosses the ball to another student. Keep tossing the ball until all the businesses have been visited. Guide the students in noticing how the yarn looks like a web. Have them jointly move the web up and down to see how it is interconnected and supported. Ask the students what would happen to the web if the yarn was thrown to a person outside the circle. Would the web be as strong? After this activity, tell each student to pick one business in your area and write a paragraph telling why the business is an important part of the community.

Day 5: Nia (Purpose) Local Biographies

The fifth day is used to discuss the achievements of ancestors and other African Americans. Contact local African American ministers, business owners, government officials, artists, and craftsmen. Make appointments for them to come and be interviewed by your students. Prior to the visits, have the students work in pairs to create lists of at least ten interview questions. Instruct the students to inquire about the individual's childhood, family life, profession, and accomplishments. Have students tape-record the interviews so they can refer to them later if needed.

After the interviews are complete, instruct the students to write short biographies of the people interviewed. Laminate the final copies and compile them into a book. Display the book in the library; then invite the people interviewed to come and see the final product.

Day 6: Kuumba (Creativity)
Karamu: The Kwanzaa Feast

This day's principle is expressed through readings, singing, dancing, and artwork. It is also the day of exchanging gifts and the big feast of Kwanzaa called *karamu.* Food is spread out on a large mkeka in the middle of the room along with the other symbols of Kwanzaa. Have the students—with the help of parent volunteers—prepare their own karamu that includes the recipes below. Other favorite foods include catfish, collard greens, black-eyed peas, and sweet potato pie. While you eat your feast, have students discuss ways they demonstrated their creativity during your Kwanzaa study.

African Sweet Potato Salad

Ingredients:
4 sweet potatoes
1/4 cup vegetable oil
2 tablespoons lemon juice
1/2 teaspoon salt
1/4 teaspoon pepper
1 chopped green pepper
1 chopped small onion
1 chopped celery stalk
parsley

Directions:
Heat 1 cup of water to boiling. Add sweet potatoes. Bring to a boil; then reduce heat and cover. Cook for about 35 minutes or until tender. Cool the potatoes and peel off skins. Cut the potatoes into cubes and put into a bowl. Combine oil, lemon juice, salt, and pepper. Pour this mixture over the potatoes. Cover and refrigerate. Before serving stir in green pepper, onion, and celery. Sprinkle with parsley. (Serves 6.)

Akwadu
(Baked Bananas And Coconuts)
A Treat From Ghana, Africa

Ingredients:
5 bananas
1 tablespoon margarine
1/3 cup orange juice
1 tablespoon lemon juice
3 tablespoons brown sugar
2/3 cup coconut

Directions:
Cut each banana into halves crosswise; then cut each half lengthwise. Put bananas in a greased 9-inch pie pan. Dab margarine on bananas; pour orange and lemon juice over them. Sprinkle bananas with brown sugar and coconut. Bake at 375° until coconut is golden brown, about 8 to 10 minutes. (Serves 5 to 6.)

Day 7: Imani (Faith)
Honor Wall

The first day of the year is the last day of Kwanzaa. This day is used to reflect on the faith an individual has in herself, her family, teachers, leaders, and race. Discuss with the students that *imani* (faith) is believing in someone or something. Have students explain what it means to be a role model. Help the students understand that a role model is a person who represents honesty, compassion, understanding, hard work, concern for others, etc. Have students create a display that honors the role models in their community, school, and families. Cover a bulletin board with bright paper and the title "Role Model Honor Wall." Duplicate a supply of the nomination forms below; then place them in a basket near the display. Let a student nominate someone for the wall by completing one of the forms, coloring its border, and stapling it to the board. If possible, post photographs of the nominees on the wall, too. Encourage other students and teachers in the school to add to your honor wall.

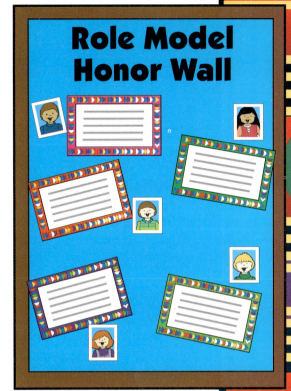

Pattern

Recognizing A Role Model

Nominee for the Role Model Honor Wall: _____

Nominated by: _____

I nominate this person for the Role Model Honor Wall because _____

_____
_____
_____
_____
_____
_____

©1996 The Education Center, Inc. • *DECEMBER* • TEC201

Nguzo Saba
(en-GOO-zoh SAH-bah)
The Seven Principles Of Kwanzaa

Day 1: Umoja (oo-MOH-jah)
Unity
Black Candle
Helping each other in the family and community.

Day 2: Kujichagulia (koo-jee-chah-goo-LEE-ah)
Self-Determination
Red Candle
Making our own decisions.

Day 3: Ujima (oo-JEE-mah)
Collective Work And Responsibility
Green Candle
Working together to make life better for one another.

Day 4: Ujamaa (oo-jah-MAH-ah)
Cooperative Economics
Red Candle
Building and supporting our own businesses.

Day 5: Nia (NEE-ah)
Purpose
Green Candle
Being aware that our lives have meaning and purpose.

Day 6: Kuumba (koo-OOM-bah)
Creativity
Red Candle
Using our imagination and hands to create.

Day 7: Imani (ee-MAH-nee)
Faith
Green Candle
Believing in ourselves, our ancestors, and our future.

©1996 The Education Center, Inc. • *DECEMBER* • TEC201

Note To The Teacher: Use with "Unity Cup" on page 85 and "Shedding Light On Kwanzaa" on page 86.

Pattern Use with "Shedding Light On Kwanzaa" on page 86.

Follow these steps:

1. Read page 92. Then complete and color each of your group's candles.
2. Cut out the candles; then cut on the short dotted lines at the bottom of each candle.
3. Fold on the fold lines. Fold the small flaps at the bottom outward.
4. Put glue on the tab; then fold the candle and attach the tab to the other end to make a triangular candle.
5. Glue the bottom flaps to the shoebox. Be sure to glue your candles in the correct order as shown in the illustration below.

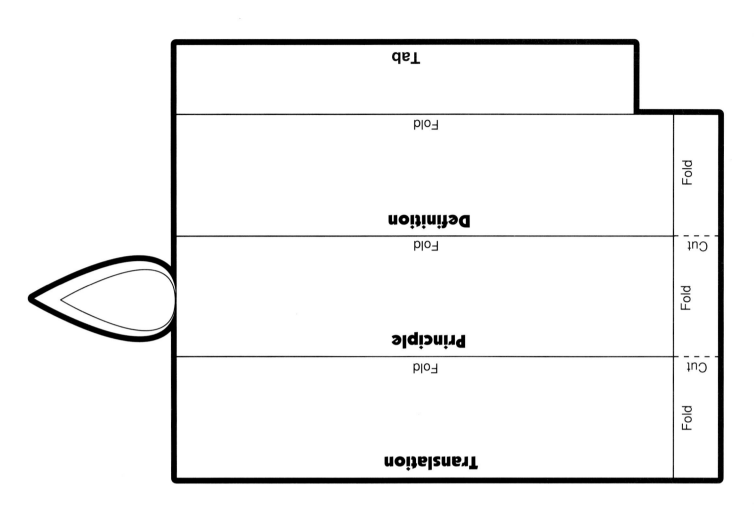

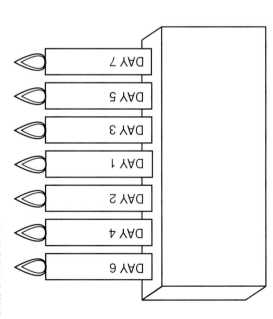

Finished Kinara

Name _____ Critical thinking

Dreams For The Future

Directions: Complete each sentence with a dream that fits your goals for the future.

In the future, I would like to change _____

In the future, I would like to live _____

In the future, I would like to see (visit) _____

In the future, I would like to be (career) _____

In the future, I would like to make the world a better place by _____

In the future, I would like to learn how to _____

Bonus Box: List ten things you can do that will help make your dreams come true.

©1996 The Education Center, Inc. • DECEMBER • TEC201

94

Note To The Teacher: Use with "Muhindi" on page 86 and "I Am Free" on page 88.

Answer Keys

Page 27
1. Saint Nicholas
2. reindeer
3. candy cane
4. Santa Claus
5. gift wrap
6. sleigh ride
7. fruitcake
8. gingerbread
9. evergreen
10. jingle bells
11. "Silent Night"
12. mistletoe
13. candlelight
14. holly wreath
15. family reunion
16. cookie cutter
17. snowflake
18. choir music

Bonus Box: plum pudding

Page 57
1. false; 24
2. false; 4
3. true; 19
4. true; 6
5. false; 7
6. true; 13
7. true; 26
8. false; 2
9. true; 5
10. true; 1
11. false; 23
12. false; 21
13. true; 16
14. false; 22
15. false; 8
16. true; 9

Boxes should spell out: BECAME PRESIDENTS

Page 38
1. 36 eggs
2. 175 boxes of cornflakes
3. 5 loaves
4. 64 ounces of bacon
5. $24.00 for bacon
6. $3.00
7. 120 quarts of milk
8. 60 more quarts of milk than orange juice
9. 28 sticks of butter for seven days or 20 sticks for five days (Accept either answer.)
10. $10.00 for bread

Bonus Box: Answers will vary.

Page 45
1. **H**EXAGRAM
2. **A**CUTE angle
3. **P**ARALLELOGRAM*
4. **P**OLYGON
5. SUPPLEMENTAR**Y** angles
6. **R**HOMBUS*
7. **T**RAPEZOID
8. **I**NTERSECT
9. CONGR**U**ENT
10. segment **KE**
11. triangle LB**K** or JI**K**
12. EQUIL**AT**ERAL triangle
13. **H**EXAGON

*Note: A *parallelogram* is a quadrilateral whose opposite sides are parallel. A *rhombus* is a parallelogram with congruent sides.

Bonus Box: Since the star has 12 sides and they are all equal, its perimeter is 36 inches.

Page 58
The rights guaranteed by the Bill of Rights include (wording of answers may vary):
1. People have freedom to worship, freedom of speech and the press, the right to assemble peacefully, and the right to petition the government for changes.
2. People have the right to keep and bear arms.
3. During peacetime, soldiers cannot be housed in a private home without the consent of the owner.
4. People or their homes may not be searched unreasonably.
5. A person accused of a serious crime has the right to a jury trial; a person cannot be tried for the same crime twice; a person cannot be forced to testify against himself; a person's life, liberty, or property cannot be taken from him without due process of law. Also, if the government takes a person's property for public use, it must pay the owner for it.
6. A person accused of a serious crime has the right to a speedy, public trial in the district where the crime was committed; the right to face his accusers; the right to call favorable witnesses; the right to have the assistance of a legal defense counselor.
7. In most cases a person has the right to a jury trial.
8. The punishment or payment required for a crime must not be cruel or unreasonable.
9. A person has other rights besides those outlined in the Constitution.
10. Any powers not specifically given to the federal government or denied to it by the states in the Constitution remain with the states or the people.

Answer Keys

Page 68
1. −24°F
2. 30 mph
3. 10 mph
4. −10°F
5. 1°F
6. between −22°F and −25°F
7. 20°F
8. 20°F when the wind speed is 30 mph and 10°F when the wind speed is 15 mph
9. −20°F and 0 mph; 20°F and 35 mph
10. zero mph

Bonus Box: The wind chill is −5°F under these four conditions:
- −5°F and zero mph
- 0°F and 5 mph
- 20°F and 15 mph
- 30°F and 40 mph

The wind chill is −10°F under these four conditions:
- −10°F and 0 mph
- −5°F and 5 mph
- 20°F and 20 mph
- 25°F and 30 mph

The wind chill is −15°F under these four conditions:
- −15°F and 0 mph
- −10°F and 5 mph
- 5°F and 10 mph
- 20°F and 25 mph

Page 69
2. The two types of snow crystals are *plates* and *columns*. Both types have six sides, but the air temperature and the amount of moisture present determine whether they take the shape of a plate or a column.
10. It takes six inches of moist snow or 30 inches of dry snow to equal the water in one inch of rain.

Page 82
1. chewing gum
2. jigsaw puzzle
3. safety pin
4. pencil
5. rubber band
6. toothbrush
7. bed
8. cereal
9. glue
10. Levi's® jeans

Page 83
Answers may vary. Accept any reasonable answer.
1. plate: things with a hole in the center
2. steel: things that stick/are sticky
3. comb: things you can sit on
4. can opener: things that project light
5. lightbulb: things that emit sound
6. aspirin: things with a lens
7. camera: things that fly/travel through the air
8. basket: things that cut
9. rubber band: things that clean
10. toothpick: things with teeth
11. canoe: things with wheels, *or* shopping cart: forms of transportation
12. television: things with adjectives as part of their names
13. telephone: things that measure
14. typewriter: things that calculate
15. clock: things that give direction